Timothy Peter

ISBN: 9781313410854

Published by:
HardPress Publishing
8345 NW 66TH ST #2561
MIAMI FL 33166-2626

Email: info@hardpress.net
Web: http://www.hardpress.net

GLANDERS

A Clinical Treatise

BY

WILLIAM HUNTING, F.R.C.V.S.

Examiner in Veterinary Science to the University of London.
Chief Veterinary Inspector to the London County Council.

LONDON :

H. & W. BROWN, 20 FULHAM ROAD, S.W.

1908.

CONTENTS.

PREFACE.

Twenty-one years ago I wrote a little book on glanders with the object of showing that farcy and glanders were one disease, and must be treated as one before legislation could have any successful effect upon its control. In the preface I claimed to "have attempted to supply the facts and arguments required to establish the assertion that glanders can be completely stamped out."

We have gone a long way since that time. No one now doubts the contagious nature of the disease. The causal organism is well-known, and what was then our great difficulty—the impossibility of diagnosing the latent form of the disease—has been removed by the discovery of mallein.

Since then legislation has been brought up to the level of veterinary science, and now all that is necessary for success is an earnest and enlightened application of the regulations issued by the Board of Agriculture.

My object in publishing this clinical monograph on Glanders is to provide those whose experience is small with such information as may assist them to detect and suppress the disease if they should meet with it.

Probably the book would never have been written had not my opportunities (including about 600 post-mortem examinations per annum for the London County Council) afforded a unique collection of glanders lesions. From these I selected typical specimens, and Mr. S. A. Sewell, of 190 Fleet Street, made water-colour drawings which have been faithfully reproduced by the Anglo Engraving Company. Mr. Sewell is a pathological artist of such skill that I was fortunate in obtaining his assistance. His work, done at the slaughter-house, so as to get the natural colour of the fresh specimen, was often unpleasant, and I am greatly indebted to him.

Every year, as glanders gradually disappears before the regulations of the Board of Agriculture and the efforts of Local Authorities, these pictures of its lesions will be more and more useful; and original specimens of the older post-mortem appearances will soon, I believe, be unobtainable.

WILLIAM HUNTING, F.R.C.V.S.

London, 1908.

GLANDERS.

SYNONYMS.   Glanders.   Farcy.   *Latin*, Malleus.   *French*, Morve. *Italian*, Morva.   *German*, Rotz.   *Dutch*, Snot.   *Danish*, Snive.

Nomenclature.   All these terms were brought into use before pathology had become a science, and their meaning is generally to be found in reference to some prominent symptom.   The terms Glanders and Farcy were used by our earliest veterinary writers, who acknowledged their introduction from either France or Italy.   They were supposed to indicate two distinct diseases, one—glanders, having its seat in the head, the other—farcy, showing itself on the skin.

The word glanders clearly referred to some change in the glands, and one of the most common symptoms of glanders is an enlargement of the submaxillary glands.   It is curious that if the term glanders was derived from the French, it should have been replaced in France by the word Morve—literally meaning snot or snotty—a direct reference to the nasal discharge which is so marked a symptom of the disease.

The term Farcy is, with slight alteration, the French word *Farcin* (from *farcere*, to stuff, cram or surfeit).   Farcy was described by Markham in 1651, whilst Farcin is the word used by Bracken as late as 1737. This form of the disease, consisting of swelling of legs and ulcers on the body, was supposed to result from humours caused by surfeit.

Considering that in the 17th century authors differentiated between strangles and glanders, and between farcy and nettlerash, it is remarkable that they detected no connection between farcy and glanders. Either form seldom proves fatal without the development of symptoms common to both.   The Dutch term "Snot" and the Danish "Snive" are clearly related to our own vulgar words "snotty" and "snivel," all indicating nasal discharge. The German term Rotz is expressive of a similar condition—the snivelling or snuffling accompanying discharge from the nose.

In the early parts of last century farriers used the terms "button" farcy, and "water" farcy. The first referred to those cases in which small round "buds" were the prominent symptom. The latter was a misnomer, as it was used to describe a different disease, known now as purpura hæmorrhagica.

Definition.   Glanders is a specific disease due to the growth and development within the animal body of a micro-organism—*Bacillus Mallei*. The disease is characterised by morbid changes affecting the skin, mucous membranes, lungs, lymphatic glands, and other organs. These changes vary according to the activity and position of the causal organism, and are modified by the health, age, and condition of the infected animal.

HISTORY.

Glanders was recognised by Hippocrates about 450 B.C., and by Aristotle a century later. It was described by Apsyrtus in the 4th century of our era, and by Vegetius in the 5th. In 1618, the celebrated Italian anatomist Ruini described glanders, and declared it to be "a general disease and incurable." In 1669, Solleysel recognised it as a contagious disease. He wrote : " This disease is more easily communicated than any other, because not only are horses in contact with diseased animals attacked—but the air itself is infected, and in this manner are infected other horses under the same roof." He got nearer the truth by the remark " Farcy is first cousin to glanders."

Gervase Markham who wrote in 1630, enumerated among the causes of glanders "standing with infected horses." He was confused in his description of the nature of the disease, and enumerates three stages or forms, concluding thus : " To these three distillations there is commonly added a fourth, which is when the matter that comes from the nose is dark, thin and reddish, but then this is Mourning of the Chine which is a disease for the most part incurable."

No writer of the 17th century expressed any clear ideas about the nature of glanders but they all seem to have observed that it was contagious, and it would have been well for horse-owners had this simple experience not been upset by theories of less acute observers.

In the 18th century some progress was made, and a French Veterinarian Gaspard de Saunier, 1734, recognised glanders as "highly contagious" and traced its transmission through harness, water troughs, pails and mangers. Unfortunately in 1749 Lafosse Senior, Farrier to the King, communicated to the French Royal Academy of Medicine "A memoir of the glanders in horses," in which he argued that the seat of the disease was in the nasal cavities, and he concluded "that glanders does not depend upon a general distemper of the blood, but is really and truly a simple and local malady." For half a century this non-contagion theory obtained general acceptance, although a few eminent veterinarians attempted to refute it. Lafosse's opinions gained weight from his prominent position, and their wide acceptance was disastrous to the adoption of any rational preventive measures.

Bourgelat, the founder of modern veterinary science, who established the schools in Paris and Lyons, was a believer in the contagious nature of the disease, but it was not till the 19th century had almost arrived that general acceptance was given to the view that glanders might be contagious; and even then another fifty years was to pass during which authorities held that although contagion played a part, yet other causes might give origin to the disease. The Lyons School and its graduates supported a contagious origin, the Paris School took the opposite view, and so prevention was neglected.

In 1773, Vitet expressed the opinion that glanders consisted in a discharge from the nose of "a virulent and contagious humour," and he stated that "the chest and the head were the seat of the disease." In the same year Volpi, of Milan, thought he noticed an analogy between syphilis and glanders, and suspected that glanders and farcy, from their frequent association, might be the same disease. He also asserted that "glanders is caused by contagion alone."

In 1797, Eric Viborg, a Danish veterinarian, published a work on glanders in which he showed that there was a specific virus in the purulent discharges of horses suffering from glanders and farcy; that farcy and glanders were one disease; that the virus could be destroyed by heat and dessication; and that infection could be carried by harness or utensils, and more particularly by forage left in mangers from which diseased horses had fed. He also recognised a latent form of disease which might be infective, and warned against the danger from horses which had been apparently cured of farcy. It is sad to think of the losses which have since occurred, and which might largely have been prevented had the work of this excellent observer been accepted. Viborg, in 1797, knew practically all that was known about glanders up to the time of the discovery of the Bacillus mallei.

In the 19th century, knowledge of glanders progressed slowly at first. Professor Coleman, who had succeeded St. Bel at the London Veterinary School, devoted much attention to glanders. He proved experimentally that farcy might be produced by inoculation of matter from acute glanders, and glanders by the inoculation of matter from farcy. He showed that the virus might exist in the blood by inducing glanders in a donkey through transfusion of blood from a glandered horse, and yet he held that the disease might originate without contagion.

Youatt believed the disease to be strictly local for awhile, that then it caused ulcers, that the suppuration became malignant and thus affected the whole system.

White, a retired army veterinary surgeon, who had entered upon private practice at Exeter, wrote in 1817 a very true account of the clinical behaviour of glanders, which he recognised as a contagious disease. White's last edition (1842), page 223, contains the following: "Glanders is a contagious disease which is communicated by inoculation, or by swallowing the matter, and not by effluvia, proceeding from a glandered horse or a stable in which a glandered horse is, or has been kept."

Blaine asserted that "both glanders and farcy originate in contagion and that the disease is one *sui generis*."

Professor Sewell in 1827, taught that the lungs were the original seat of disease, and the affection of the nose secondary. He believed that the miliary tubercles in the lung constitute the original disease.

Between the years 1830 and 1840, a great deal of work on glanders was done in France, but still the Paris and Lyons Schools held to their opposite views concerning contagion. Renault, Delafond, and Bouley accepted the spontaneous origin as proved, and their views obtained wide acceptance in Germany, Italy and England.

Leblanc contributed to the morbid anatomy of glanders, and gave a full description of the lesions found. He taught that glanders and farcy are the same disease, that the nodules in the lungs are not tuberculous—but specific, and described them as "commencing by red points, whose centres in time turn white, remaining for a while enveloped in a red case. At length the enclosed matter becomes softened, then hardens again and turns of a calcareous nature."

About this time the transmission of glanders from horse to man was recognised. Schilling, a German observer, had reported in 1821 the death of a soldier from glanders—probably the first indubitable case published. Travers published in 1830 a case in which a veterinary student had died of glanders in 1817. The true nature of the disease was proved by inoculation of two donkeys, and it is interesting to know that Professor Coleman, of the London Veterinary School, was associated with Travers in the investigation of the case. It is a pity to have to add that these investigators failed to recognise the significance of their experiments and regarded this and other human cases as the result merely of cadaveric poisoning. In 1833, Elliotson published in the *Medico-Chirurgical Transactions*, an account of two cases of his own, and others he had collected, which established the transmissibility. In 1837, Rayer published an account of a case of human glanders from which he reproduced the disease in a horse by inoculation of pus from his patient. This had a wide effect in France in converting men to a belief in the contagious nature of the disease.

In 1840, a series of experiments were made by Renault and Bouley, at Alfort, which established, beyond a doubt, that glanders was contagious; and since then very few men have ventured to deny that glanders may be transmitted by contagion. But many have believed that it might arise from other causes, such as the introduction into a horse's system of purulent fluids, or even by changes in the blood resulting from defective hygienic conditions.

In 1858, William Percival published his well-known work on " Hippo-pathology—a systematic treatise on the disorders and lameness of the horse." In Volume III. is an article on Glanders, extending to 200 pages, and embracing a most careful and extensive review of the work done on the disease by every writer from Solleysel downwards. No less than forty authors are quoted and analysed, but very few contributed much useful information. Of this history I have made use in compiling these pages.

Percival himself says on page 239: "I have no more doubt of glanders being a contagious disease, than I have of syphilis or small-pox or itch being contagious." He then proceeds to discuss the opinions of other authorities as to the origin of the disease, and says: "No doubt has ever been entertained by me of the spontaneous origin of glanders and farcy—of their origin, apart from the influence of contagion." Further on we find: "Of the nature of the (so-called) virus of glanders we know no more than we do concerning the supposed viruses or poisons of syphilis, rabies, or variolus. We have the same ground for arguing the existence of virus, as there is for doing so in the diseases just named, and no more. . . . We do not imagine that simply an unhealthy or ill-conditioned state of body can give rise to glanders or farcy. We believe that the specific virus must, in some form or another, somewhere or other exist." Percival also recognised that: "the poison of glanders after its absorption may be latent, or in the system for weeks—months even—the same as the virus of syphilis is known on occasions to be, and as that of rabies always is."

For many years after Percival wrote, the views expressed by him were generally accepted, and few practitioners disbelieved in the occasional spontaneous origin of glanders. "Miasmas" or "mephitic vapours" arising from bad ventilation and over-crowding, tempered by climatic changes of an indefinite kind, were the assumed cause of outbreaks which could not be traced directly to contagion. Thus practical measures of prevention were neglected, or limited to the isolation of the most marked cases. Not until Pasteur, in 1863, had demonstrated that every living organism arose only as the result of a similar previous organism, did the theory of spontaneous origin of contagious disease yield to observation and argument. Much useful work on the pathology and morbid anatomy of glanders was contributed by Rayer, Leblanc, Bouley, Gerlach, Leisering and Chauveau.

In 1882, the causal organism—Bacillus mallei, was isolated and cultivated in France by Bouchard, Capitan and Charrin, and about the same time, independently by Loeffler and Schütz in Germany.

In 1891, the Russian veterinary surgeons, Helman and Kalning obtained from sterilised cultures of the bacillus a product called Mallein, which possesses the remarkable property of causing a specific reaction when injected into glandered horses—but which has no effect in horses free from glanders. Schütz, Roux, Nocard, M'Fadyean, Kitt, and Babes have since added considerably to our knowledge, and Governments in various parts of the world have issued regulations for the control of glanders based upon the results of veterinary observation and scientific research. During the years 1891-92, no less than seven European scientists working at glanders lost their lives through accidental infection.

DISTRIBUTION AND PREVALENCE.

Glanders has been distributed by trade or war to every country in the world. In Europe it has been known for centuries. In India and China probably as long. All the great wars have increased its prevalence, and often carried it into districts where before it was unknown. In the Crimea glanders prevailed widely. In the Italo-Austrian, in the Franco-Prussian, and in the Civil War of the United States, glanders prevailed not only during the wars, but even more actively after peace was made, by the movement and dispersal of superfluous horses.

Our minor wars in Egypt, Abyssinia and Afghanistan were all attended by glanders to an extent which interfered with efficiency. The United States are said to have introduced glanders into Mexico and Cuba with their army horses. The South African War, where 240,000 horses perished, was not only accompanied by the prevalence of glanders, but left the whole country infected. The disease was carried to South Africa from home, from America and Australia, and possibly from Europe, by the remounts.

By trade we have received glanders from the United States, Canada and Europe, and we have returned it. The trade in old horses to Belgium has introduced glanders to that country frequently. Probably no civilized country on the face of the earth is now free from the disease.

In Great Britain few counties remain free for any length of time, but the disease chiefly prevails in the large towns—in London and Glasgow especially.

No statistics as to the prevalence of glanders are available before the year 1870, and the returns for that year, made to the Privy Council under the Contagious Diseases (Animals) Act of 1869, are quite misleading, not a tenth of the cases then existing being reported. In 1874, the returns became a little more exact by the inclusion of farcy—a form of the disease not recognised as necessary for legal control in 1869. By about the year 1881, I think, the returns began to fairly represent the prevalence of disease, and we may now accept the annual figures of the Board of Agriculture as practically correct.

The following Table shows the number of horses attacked with glanders since 1887. The total number 40,936, valued at £20 a head, discloses the frightful loss which has been sustained by horse-owners in twenty-one years—not less than £818,720.

TABLE I.

HORSES ATTACKED WITH GLANDERS IN GREAT BRITAIN, 1887 TO 1907.

Year.	No. attacked.	Year.	No. attacked.
1887	1482	1898	1385
1888	1581	1899	1472
1889	2246	1900	1858
1890	1808	1901	2370
1891	2435	1902	2040
1892	3001	1903	2499
1893	2133	1904	2658
1894	1437	1905	2068
1895	1594	1906	2012
1896	1294	1907	1934
1897	1629		
			40,936

Outbreaks of glanders, as of other contagious diseases, vary in number year by year, but show no regular periodicity. The increase of disease depends upon conditions which favour the development and transmission of the bacilli—such as the extra movements of horses by trade or war, excessive work and fatiguing weather. After a maximum year of prevalence, we generally find a fall continuing through two or three years. This may be accounted for by the greater activity displayed by owners and authorities, who have been alarmed by the heavy losses. It may also be partly due to a number of latent cases having been developed by the general conditions which accounted for the increased prevalence, and so leaving fewer infected horses to "break-up" in succeeding years.

The chart Table II. shows the fluctuations of glanders over some years.

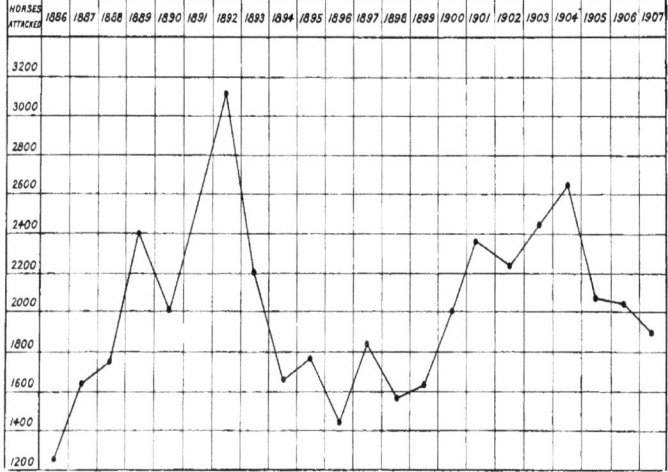

During the last ten years, a factor of unknown effect upon the distribution of the disease has been introduced in the form of mallein. By its use owners can detect disease before it is evidenced by any symptoms, and they may then sell the latently infected horse and so spread glanders to distant parts of the country. On the other hand, mallein used under the control of local authorities has been the means of increasing the notification by numbers of cases which would, in the natural course of time, not have been detected for months later. Probably the last three or four years show the comparatively large returns of horses attacked more from the number of mallein reactors reported than from any increase in the prevalence of disease.

TABLE III.

PREVALENCE IN COUNTIES—TEN YEARS TO 1901, AND 1907.

COUNTIES.	1892	1893	1894	1895	1896	1897	1898	1899	1900	1901
dford	...	7	...	1	1	5	6	1	2	4
rks	1	...	8	2	1	...	1	2	1	4
ckingham	2	4	10	2	1	2	12	5	5	8
mbridge	3	5	4	16	...	...	...	12	13	14
iester	10	10	5	21	11	6	5	6	2	2
rnwall	...	...	...	...	...	...	...	...	...	...
imberland	...	...	...	4	13	...	...	...	...	1
rby	...	...	...	2	...	2	2	22	3	1
von	1	...	...	...	...	1	...	...	...	1
rset	...	...	4	...	1	...	...	...	1	...
irham	1	2	1	9	28	8	...	7	3	1
sex	70	55	52	81	49	57	49	62	75	119
oucester	...	6	...	...	3	22	...	...	...	3
ints	12	6	7	8	...	1	2	3	8	2
reford	...	...	...	...	...	...	...	...	...	3
rtford	14	28	19	8	18	11	12	11	8	16
intingdon	4	2	13	1	...	...	...	...	...	...
nt	26	28	19	18	21	24	8	12	39	51
ncashire	14	24	10	44	52	34	24	38	14	21
icester	...	...	...	...	...	1	...	1	...	...
ncoln	2	3	...	...	1	...	1	1	1	1
ndon	2526	1619	1093	1042	845	966	800	896	1387	1828
ddlesex	121	121	82	109	52	73	94	77	96	93
nmouth	...	...	...	6	...	...	...	...	...	...
rfolk	4	3	3	3	...	15	14	10	39	6
rthampton	...	4	...	6	1	...	2	1	13	6
rthumberland	...	2	...	1	21	3	...	16	19	2
tts	1	1	...	...	1	15	...	1	...	1
ford	7	1	1	...	...	...	...	2	1	...
tland	...	...	...	...	...	...	...	...	...	...
lop	...	1	...	1	1	...	...	...	...	1
merset	1	...	...	...	...	...	...	2	6	1
fford	11	12	8	22	3	1	1	1	8	5
ffolk	4	...	6	1	...	9	1	7	...	6
rrey	35	45	16	23	26	20	9	20	22	17
ssex	4	8	6	11	5	7	3	19	8	44
irwick	14	42	16	32	19	21	21	15	15	15
estmoreland	2	2	...	1	...	...	...	3	...	...
lts	2	1	...	1	...	...	2	...	...	7
rcester	3	4	3	...	2	4	1	3	3	...
rk	21	12	14	11	20	16	3	13	...	3
les	6	4	2	1	...	8	1	...	...	2
tland	79	71	134	106	98	297	251	203	41	64

In London this year, 1908, no less than 70 per cent. of the cases returned, are those detected by mallein under the regulations of the New Order.

Table III. was compiled some years ago, but is still available to show the comparative prevalence of disease in English counties; I have merely added the year 1907 for comparison. Ireland may be left out of the question, as glanders is only found there when an infected horse has been imported—a very infrequent event. The table shows that London is the most important centre of the disease, and that the counties immediately bordering upon it are the next great sufferers. Mining and manufacturing districts come next; whilst purely agricultural counties are only temporarily infected by the introduction of a horse suffering from disease. As a rule, the isolated outbreaks do not involve more than two or three horses before they are stamped out by the authorities. There is one practical fact about this distribution of glanders which should be emphasised—viz.: that the purchase of young horses from English country districts entails no risk, but the purchase of old horses in London for work in the country is at present inadvisable, unless their condition is tested by an early injection of mallein.

TABLE IV.

PREVALENCE OF GLANDERS IN LONDON AND SURROUNDING COUNTIES
COMPARED WITH REST OF ENGLAND.

Year.	London	Middx.	Essex	Kent	Surrey	Hert-ford	Sussex	Total	Total in whole of England.	Per cent.
1895	1042	109	81	18	23	8	11	1292	1487	86·8
96	845	52	49	21	26	18	5	1016	1196	84·9
97	966	73	57	24	20	11	7	1158	1324	87·4
98	860	94	49	8	9	12	3	1035	1133	91·3
99	896	77	62	12	20	11	19	1097	1269	95·5
1900	1387	96	75	39	22	8	8	1635	1814	95·6
1901	1828	93	119	51	17	3	44	2155	2304	93·5

The above table shows at a glance the prevalence of glanders in and around London, and the relative proportions of the disease in the metropolitan district and the rest of England.

That London infects the surrounding counties is beyond dispute, but it must also be acknowledged that many cases are found in the Metropolis which have come from neighbouring districts where they were infected.

The prevalence of glanders varies, not only year by year, but month by month, and the following table shows the fluctuations in London for five years. From July to October inclusive we find the greatest amount of disease, and from February to April the least.

TABLE V.

PREVALENCE OF GLANDERS IN LONDON MONTH BY MONTH.

	1897	1898	1899	1900	1901	Total	Average per month for 5 years.
January	69	70	69	105	179	492	98
February	64	59	44	121	129	417	83
March	81	60	63	111	126	441	88
April	83	63	61	116	124	447	89
May	71	83	56	120	161	491	98
June	76	93	61	91	129	447	89
July	99	82	82	110	164	537	107
August	86	76	83	136	196	577	115
September	103	77	124	132	173	609	121
October	102	70	77	110	159	518	103
November	75	59	107	121	143	505	101
December	71	53	78	114	166	482	96

The explanation I offer of this fluctuation is that the hot months of the year are the most exhausting, and that fatigue causes premature development of the disease which might otherwise have continued latent in its pulmonary form. I assume that all visible cases of glanders have previously suffered from nodules in the lungs for at least two or three, and possibly for 12 months. I know that a febrile condition, especially when accompanied by pulmonary congestion, frequently determines generalisation of the disease, and then the clinical symptoms appear. The summer and autumn seasons are those in which unfavourable conditions for the inhibition of glanders prevail.

ETIOLOGY.

Glanders arises from one cause only—the presence of the micro-organism *Bacillus mallei* in the system of an animal.

There are conditions and influences which modify, retard, or favour the development of the bacillus, and these are worthy of some considera-tion, as they have a very practical bearing on the development and spread of the disease.

In 1882, Loeffler and Schütz, in Germany, discovered the bacillus, so too, about the same time did Bouchard, Capitan and Charrin, working independently in France. They isolated it, cultivated it, and produced glanders in animals by inoculation of the culture.

The bacilli are found in the discharges from glanders lesions, in unopened farcy buds, and in the nodules formed in internal organs. In the lungs the most recent nodules afford the larger number of active bacilli.

The microbes are rod-shaped organisms, about 3 to 5 micro-millimetres in length by 1 in breadth. The extremities are rounded. The bacilli are non-motile, can be stained by suitable re-agents, but are not very retentive of the stain. They can be cultivated in suitable media in the presence of air and at temperatures varing from 75 F. to 103 F. They cease to grow at 112, and below 60 F. At 130 F. they are killed. Upon agar, the colonies form a whitish layer. Upon potato, there forms a yellowish honeylike layer which becomes gradually darker, varying from light brown to chocolate. The formation of spores has not been demonstrated. These cultures, when inoculated into susceptible animals, are more virulent than any products of the natural glanders lesions. Accidentally men have been infected by needles and syringes which had been used for experimental inoculation of animals, and in every case death from acute glanders followed. "Horses, asses, mules, cats, goats, field mice and guinea pigs have all been infected. Rabbits, sheep and dogs are slightly suscep-tible. Cattle, swine and white mice have an immunity" (Crookshank).

By passing the bacilli through different animals, their virulence may be decreased or increased, and it is said that the microbe becomes most virulent in man.

Sub-cultures rapidly lose their virulence.   The bacillus can, with difficulty, be isolated from the blood.   It probably does not retain its vitality long in the blood-stream, but that it exists there in acute cases is shown by the successful production of glanders by transfusion of blood from a diseased into a healthy animal.

The bacilli of glanders are killed by exposure to bright sunlight, by desiccation, and by a temperature of over 130 F.   They remain active for about 18 days in clean water, and cannot retain their vitality out of an animal body or a bacteriological laboratory for more than three months— seldom over six weeks.   Most disinfectants destroy the bacillus rapidly. A 5 per cent solution of Carbolic Acid, or a solution of Corrosive Subli- mate 1 to 1000, are quite reliable.   Lysol, Permanganate of Potass, Chinosol, and many others may also be used.

Influences affecting Infection.   As some species of animals are immune to glanders and as some have a partial immunity—so some horses, if not altogether immune, show a strong resistance.   When it was permis- sible to treat cases of glanders and farcy, there were instances of apparent recovery after the exhibition of clinical symptoms.   Many horses made partial recoveries, and some recovered and worked for years without ever showing any further sign of disease.   Horses have frequently been known to work with, and to stand in the stables alongside visibly glandered horses and yet never show a sign of infection.   The most probable explanation is that they were infected, but did not develop the disease. I am inclined to doubt whether any horse was ever sufficiently resistive to be immune to a full dose of glanders virus such as exists in a pure culture, but my experience warrants me in saying that numbers of horses naturally infected have lived and worked for years without giving evidence of their infection.

Age has a decided influence on the susceptibility.   Old horses with- stand the disease to a marked extent.   Young horses are easily infected, and the period is short before they give visible signs of their condition. Over-worked or badly fed horses are easily infected, and have no resistance to the rapid development of the bacilli.   The most resistant horse is the animal in sound, hard condition.

Other influences which affect the development of glanders are some drugs, debilitating diseases, chills and injuries. So well-known was the influence of excessive doses of physic, that in suspected cases where no clinical symptoms were visible, it used to be a common practice to administer a full dose of aloes. The superpurgation which followed was often accompanied by the signs of glanders.

Following upon influenza or acute chest affections, glanders commonly develops if the patient be suffering from the latent disease. Wounds and injuries are frequently the cause of latent glanders awakening into active disease. In a stud where latent glanders existed, it was no uncommon event to have farcy in a leg following upon injury to the foot by a nail in shoeing. That the injured part should be the first to show symptoms of the disease is, I believe, explainable on the supposition that in chronic cases of glanders, every now and then there is an escape from the lungs of stray bacilli which get into the circulation but soon perish if no suitable place for lodgment is found. A suitable place is found in injured tissues, and then the bacillus is detained and actively develops, giving rise to definite lesions.

That acute lung diseases may hasten development of glanders when active nodules are in the lungs I think is certain, but it is also true that pulmonary glanders, which has existed for months without any indication of its presence, may give rise to pleurisy and pneumonia. At a post-mortem examination, when acute pleurisy and old standing glanders lesions are found, I know no way of distinguishing by naked eye examination whether the pleurisy is specific or otherwise.

Susceptibility of different animals. As I have said before, nearly all warm blooded animals are susceptible to glanders infection except the ox, pig, and white mouse. The ass is particularly susceptible to infection, and generally succumbs rapidly to an acute attack of the disease. Chronic cases of glanders in the donkey are almost unknown. The mule is easily infected and the resulting disease is usually rapid. It takes a sort of intermediate position between the horse and ass. The larger carnivora have suffered from glanders by the ingestion of uncooked flesh of glandered horses. The disease in these animals was probably produced by flesh from sub-acute cases of equine glanders, as the blood in chronic cases does not seem dangerous. I have seen more than one horse-slaughterer gash his hand whilst cutting up glandered carcases and no infection followed. At one time it was quite usual to keep pigs and goats in large stables which were badly infected with glanders. They had access to food left by infected horses suffering from a nasal discharge, but I never knew a pig infected. Only one goat in my experience presented symptoms of glanders—it died, and the diagnosis was not confirmed by a post-mortem examination. Dogs are very resistant, no case having been reported of natural infection. By inoculation, a local sore is produced which heals spontaneously without producing a general infection.

Man suffers both from the chronic and acute form of glanders, and may be infected either by ingestion or inoculation.

Period of Incubation. This expression is generally understood to mean the time which elapses between the date of infection and the appearance of the disease. When horses are infected by direct inoculation of active virus from a glandered animal, they give evidence of infection in from three to five days. The local sore becomes angry and ulcerous, whilst the lymphatic vessels are distended and the nearest lymphatic glands enlarged.

When horses are naturally infected, or when experimentally given glanders virus in their food or water, no evident symptoms of disease are noticed for some weeks, or it may be months. Recent experiments, done with more care than was taken a generation back, suggest that infection takes place and produces some constitutional disturbance, though slight and temporary, long before the visible appearance of external symptoms. The daily use of the clinical thermometer after infection frequently indicates a rise of temperature in a few days. A post-mortem examination discloses nodules in the lungs.

In natural infection the usual period of incubation—that is the time between the reception of the virus and the appearance of clinical symptoms —is from one to three months; but in many cases much longer. The fact is that although after infection no clinical symptoms may arise for an indefinite time, glanders lesions are being formed in the lung, and this latent pulmonary disease may, according to the state of the horse, and the influences affecting him, develop slowly or rapidly, and in some cases cease to develop.

Methods of Infection. As the only cause of glanders is the Bacillus mallei, no case can arise except by the passage of the bacillus from a diseased to a healthy animal. Of course, the passage need not be direct. The bacillus may leave its habitat and remain on some place or material from which it may reach the system of an animal. So long as it retains its vitality out of the body it may be infective. Thus it is that the exact way in which the disease is spread is often involved in doubt. A glandered horse may leave infective material on food or in water and pass on. The food or water may not be consumed by a healthy horse for some time after, and the connection between the infecting and infected horse is never known, but is none the less real.

Horses suffer from glanders lesions which may be open or closed. A farcy bud on the skin allows no escape of bacilli until it is opened. A glanders nodule in the lung is for a time closed, and only when some change occurs in it do bacilli escape—it may be into lymph vessels or it may be into bronchi. In the one case they may pass from the bronchi up the respiratory passages and set up ulcerations on the mucous membrane; in the other they escape into the lymph stream, and if not soon detained to form fresh centres of infection in the lung, they reach the circulation and may give rise to lesions in any part of the body.

The open lesions of glanders are those in the air passages—trachea, larynx, and nose; and on the skin, "buds" or tumours which have broken and ulcerated. The discharges from these contain the virus, which spreads infection, either directly or indirectly, to healthy horses.

I was rash enough a few years ago to express the opinion that a horse was not infective until clinical symptoms were developed. That was a grave error, because it overlooked the possibility of the escape from the lungs of bacilli which might be coughed or sneezed out with the nasal mucus. It also overlooked a dangerous condition, not uncommon in latent glanders, in which tracheal ulceration exists without giving any evidence of its presence. Tracheal ulceration is set up by the escape through a bronchus of bacilli from the pulmonary nodules. It probably does not exist long before being accompanied by ulceration of the nasal membrane and by a nasal discharge, but it may remain uncomplicated by nasal ulceration for two or three days—more than enough time to allow infection of others before the diseased animal gives evidence of its dangerous condition.

There are three ways by which the virus may enter the body. (1) Through the skin or mucous membrane, (2) through the air passages by inhalation, and (3) by ingestion through the digestive tract.

Direct experiment has demonstrated that susceptible animals may be infected with certainty through the skin or mucous membrane if these are injured.   Inoculation introduces the material through the skin.   An abraded surface permits infection to pass through, but it is very doubtful if a sound membrane or skin does allow the infection of glanders to pass. Successful infection by rubbing-in virulent matter has been attained, but the rubbing may have destroyed the structure of the protecting surface. Abrasions and wounds have frequently afforded access to the poison of glanders.   Splinters of wood from an old manger that has been used by a glandered horse might be infected, and then penetrate the skin of the lips of another horse.   Sores might be inoculated by virus accidentally transferred on saddles and bridles.   A glandered horse, by licking or biting might infect a healthy horse.   It has often happened that disease has been transmitted by cloths or sponges used on an unrecognised case of glanders and then employed to clean or foment wounds on a healthy horse.

Direct experiment has also demonstrated the certainty with which glanders can be conveyed through food and water recently contaminated by virus from a diseased animal.   Viborg, in 1793, recognised this fact by clinical observation.   Simonds gave water containing glanders matter to healthy horses and transmitted the disease.   Renault and Bouley, in 1840, obtained the same results.   All these early experimenters laboured under the possible fallacy of their experimental subjects being already infected before being made to swallow the virulent material. No such error could vitiate the experiments of Schütz, Nocard and M'Fadyean, who all tested their subjects with mallein before proceeding. These experimenters used pure cultures, and passed them into the stomach with precautions against any accidental inoculation of the mouth, pharynx or œsophagus. They successfully infected their subjects, and could always find glanders nodules in the lungs, though seldom any lesions in other organs.

From my own clinical observations, I long ago arrived at the conviction that not only is infection possible by ingestion, but that this mode of introducing the poison is by far the most common in practice. In a cab stable where two horses work a cab but stand in different stables—a night stable and a day stable—the disease in one is usually followed by infection of the other, the most direct medium being the nose-bag. In ordinary stables, a detected case of glanders is usually followed by the appearance of disease in the horses standing on either side of the diseased one. The transmission of glanders by a common water-trough, or by pails, in stables where glandered horses are kept and worked, has been noticed and recorded frequently.

As to infection by inhalation through the air passages, it was the suggestion that seemed plausible when the virus of disease was thought to be a vapour. We now know that all viruses are particulate, and that they can only be carried through the air as dust is carried. Then the fact that cases of glanders, almost without exception, showed lung lesions, often of some age and sometimes with no other lesion, was interpreted as evidence of direct contamination of the lungs. It was argued that the frequency of lung lesions pointed to their being the primary site of infection, and that just as coal dust or stone dust could reach the lungs of miners or stone-masons by inhalation, so the glanders bacilli could enter the lungs of a horse. The most direct route to the lungs was assumed to be through the respiratory passages. The inhalation theory seemed to derive some support from the fact that intestinal or mesenteric lesions are rare in glandered horses. It was argued that these lesions would be evident if ingestion were the usual way of infection, and that the absence of abdominal lesions showed that the poison had not entered by this route. It is now known that intestinal lesions may be apparent very shortly after infection, but that they soon heal and leave only the pulmonary nodules as permanent effects.

It is beyond doubt that glanders bacilli may pass through the stomach and reach the lungs, leaving no trace of their line of progression, but giving rise to unmistakeable evidence of their arrival. The bacilli of glanders escape from the nose of an infected horse with pus or mucus in a wet condition, and are not long floating in the air. They fall upon mangers, walls, forage, water, and so are ready for ingestion. If they become dry, they must be detached from the surface on which they are dried before being capable of floating free. Dessication is fatal to the bacillus. Even supposing a few chance bacilli retain their vitality and, floating in the air, are drawn with the breath into a horse's nose, how many are likely to escape detention by the moist passages of the nose, pharynx, larynx and trachea, and to gain access to the lung? The analogy of the miner and the coal dust is not applicable. The air which caused miner's lung was absolutely full of suspended particles, and improved ventilation in mines has rendered miner's lung a rare curiosity. How many glanders bacilli, dry but vital, could be found in a cubic yard of air in the most frightfully infected stable is a metaphysical puzzle incapable of solution. An argument in favour of inhalation as a mode of infection has been founded on the fact that it is not uncommon to find cases of glanders appear in different parts of a stable so separate from each other that infection through the air is the only means of explanation. The reply is, first, that such a condition is less common than finding cases close to each other; and second, that a very simple explanation does exist. On the last occasion this fact was adduced to me as proof of aerial carriage of infection, I carefully enquired into the history of each infected horse. The diseased horses which had been slaughtered and the few that remained were certainly in very widely separated stalls. Result of enquiry was to find that the two first detected stood in certain stalls, and that every one of those that followed had been stabled next to, or near them, but had been moved for various reasons to the places in which they stood when detected. The outbreak extended over six months, and this unfortunate movement of horses had been overlooked.

It may be added that experimental attempts to produce glanders through aerial infection have never been successful. Perhaps tuberculosis is a disease about which an even more positive theory of spread by inhalation has been accepted. Guinea-pigs were made to live in air laden with dust and dry bacilli. They became infected, but no experiment was so conducted that the probability of ingestion was eliminated and inhalation alone ensured. The most recent experiments and observations point to as great a probability of fallacy here as in glanders. I am quite convinced that nearly every case of glanders has arisen as the result of the virus entering the system by ingestion.

Methods of Spread. I have just attempted to show how the infective virus of glanders leaves a diseased horse, and how it enters the system of a healthy one. The fact that the virus remains active outside the body of an animal for at least some days renders it necessary to keep observation—not only upon the diseased horse, but upon the various ways in which infection may be carried. Most important of all is it to know that a horse, apparently quite healthy, may be a source of infection. The latent form of glanders is probably not infective until some open lesion occurs, but this may happen without warning. Ulcerative lesions may arise in the trachea, rendering the horse infective, and afford no clinical evidence of existence until they have largely developed—a dangerous condition extending over some days, during which time the horse is excessively dangerous to all around him, but is unsuspected.

Then, again, visible disease may not be recognised. Although a very evident nasal discharge exists, it may be mistaken for catarrh, and so mangers and pails are infected, and other horses are allowed to use them. Every nasal discharge should be looked upon with suspicion until its nature is satisfactorily diagnosed. Sponges, leathers, combs and brushes may carry the disease from one horse to another, if they are used upon an infected animal. Of course, precautions would be taken if it were known that a diseased horse were on the premises, but latent disease is not recognisable, and it so suddenly develops in many cases that contagion is carried before it is known to be present.

There are in London many infected studs. Bankruptcy and death cause the sale of these; and the owners, without selling a single developed case of disease, often spread infection to many centres by distributing horses suffering from latent glanders.

Sale yards do not spread disease by being infected places, or by disposing of visibly infected horses. The proprietors are most careful, and much more likely to reject a horse for some symptom of an innocent nature than to sell an animal diseased. They are, however, the innocent cause of spreading glanders by disposing of horses in whose system latent glanders exists. Until mallein is used on the whole of the in-contact animals in every stable in which glanders is known to exist, we must inevitably have fresh outbreaks of disease when the latent cases develop.

In large studs having many different stables, glanders is spread to a great extent by the constant changes of horses from stable to stable to suit the exigencies of business. When once infection is introduced to such a stud, the changes of horses spread the disease to every stable unless very careful measures are taken to prevent it.

Newly purchased horses are a frequent means by which glanders is brought into a stable. Purchasers who confine themselves to young horses from the country seldom introduce glanders, but men who buy aged town horses are never long before they have the misfortune to get an infected horse.

A horse put up at livery may eat out of a manger which has been used by a glandered horse. A healthy horse may stand next to a diseased one in a shoeing forge, or in a railway horse-box. Drivers of horses may change nosebags, and one of the horses be glandered. Horses may be turned out to grass in the autumn and there meet with an infected animal. I once saw five visibly glandered horses in a field with thirty others. Probably those animals belonged to ten different owners, and ten different stables would ultimately become infected.

In no small stud does glanders remain long, because it soon kills all the horses. The disseminating centres are the large studs, and the spread from them is by the cast horses with latent disease which are purchased by the poorer owners and not suspected till too late.

From the following table I infer that 67 per cent. of glanders in London occurs as the result of continuous infection in studs which are never clear of the disease. The 32 per cent. of cases which are found in studs where no previous case has been detected are more difficult to explain. They are nearly all due to the purchase of horses suffering from the undeveloped disease, and if traceable would be found to have come from some of the permanently diseased studs, or to have been infected at grass, or possibly through public water-troughs.

TABLE VI.

RETURN SHOWING THE INCIDENCE OF 1000 CASES OF GLANDERS IN THE COUNTY OF LONDON DURING APRIL TO NOVEMBER, 1901.

Occurrence.	Number.	Per Cent.
Cases occurring in studs where there has been continuous infection for 5 or more years	389	38·9
Cases occurring in studs where there has been an occasional outbreak of infection during three years	285	28·5
Cases occurring in studs where there has been no previous case	326	32·6
	1000	

From town to town glanders is conveyed by infected horses which have not yet developed the disease in a visible form. Margate, Brighton, Worthing, Cambridge, are some of the towns into which glanders has been taken, to my own personal knowledge, by infected horses from London.

Out of the way places—villages and farms—have become mysteriously infected, and some such cases have been directly traced to travelling shows, circuses and gipsies. Of course, all sales, fairs and markets may disseminate infected horses. The way to prevent them is—not to close the yards and markets, but to look after the infected animals, and detect the latent cases.

One method of spread I must specially refer to—the public water-trough. It is quite possible that some cases of glanders have arisen as the direct effect of drinking at a public-trough, but they are very few and far between. I have an intimate knowledge of the stables of three contractors who have had, during the last twenty years, four outbreaks of glanders in their studs. Each outbreak was clearly and directly traceable to the purchase of a horse from an infected stud, and was stamped out at once without spreading. Save these outbreaks, no glanders has troubled them, and yet their horses travel all over London and drink at any water-trough they can reach. I feel convinced that infection from water-troughs is very rare, because in 90 per cent. of all outbreaks which I have personally investigated other methods of infection are traceable.

Even if 5 per cent. of all outbreaks in London were traceable to the water-troughs, the gravity of the risk would be no argument in favour of closing the troughs—especially in summer. The harm resulting to horses from being denied water all day would cause a mortality greater than is caused by all the glanders in the metropolis. The fact that an occasional case of glanders may be due to public water-troughs is an argument for the extermination of the disease, but not for closing the troughs.

The spread of glanders from country to country by war and commerce is a very serious matter. We have imported the disease from Canada and from the United States. We have exported it to Holland and Belgium. Our wars have carried it from India to Egypt, from Liverpool to Cape Town.

Most Governments are becoming alive to this danger, and are enforcing regulations against the importation of disease. Ordinary inspection at the ports will do good by suggesting to importers the risk of detection and the loss which would follow—but the mallein test is the only sure means for thorough protection.

SYMPTOMS.

Although there are cases in which the symptoms of glanders may well be described as acute, and others in which they may be called chronic, the difference is only one of degree, dependent upon the activity of the bacilli, or the resisting power of the horse. If we divided the disease into acute and chronic, we should have to add another division—sub-acute—which would probably include more of the cases seen in practice than the other two forms added together. I do not therefore propose to give separate descriptions of the two conditions. Again, glanders may appear in the cutaneous form or in the nasal form, but it is superfluous and erroneous to divide a description of symptoms into those of Glanders and of Farcy. In many cases the symptoms are mixed, but the cutaneous form seldom or never kills without the advent of other lesions.

There are symptoms of a preliminary nature which would attract the notice of an experienced stableman, but they may also be seen when glanders is not the cause and, therefore, are only suggestive. They become indicative when seen in a stud that has been contaminated by well marked cases of disease.

Loss of Energy may appear without any apparent cause, and without loss of appetite. It may be temporary, but recurrent. Probably it is only noticed by the driver, who complains that a previously energetic horse has now to be encouraged with the whip.

Wasting of the body—food and work remaining unaltered, is another symptom which should attract notice.

Cough—short, hollow, and provoked by exertion, should suggest enquiry for some definite cause.

Grunting—when the horse is turned round or when threatened, is usually a symptom of "roaring," but it is exhibited in most chest affections of a painful nature. When detected in a horse which is not feverish and not a "roarer," and when accompanied by signs of pain on pressure in the intercostal spaces, it is suspicious.

Polyuria—excessive secretion of urine, is another symptom seen frequently in advance of the generalisation of glanders. It is also sometimes noticed in tuberculosis. When only one horse in a stud shows this symptom, it may be looked upon as suspicious.

The Temperature, as indicated by a clinical thermometer, is very indicative. Whenever a horse with apparently no definite disease shows a fluctuating temperature, rising to 102˙5 F., and falling a degree or two only to rise again, glanders or tuberculosis may be suspected. In some cases the temperature remains pretty constantly at 102, with occasional rises to 103. Such horses may work and give little other indication of anything abnormal, but they should be put under close observation and rested. We now test such horses with mallein, but in the days when that agent was unknown, a constant use of the clinical thermometer in an infected stud was a useful but tedious method of picking out and isolating horses, which were then carefully watched. Many cases in time showed development of other symptoms, which proved the value of the thermometric index.

In clinically visible glanders there is always a rise of temperature, and in acute cases it may reach 107 F., when, of course, constitutional

disturbance is also well marked. In chronic cases the temperature varies
a great deal and may not rise over 102, but as a rule it is higher. The
temperature does not seem to be proportionate, either to the extent of
glanderous lesions in the lungs, or to the amount of ulcerative change in
the air passages, although, of course, when this is excessive, a rise of
temperature always exists. I incline to think that the fever in glanders
depends upon the escape from open lesions of the products of the causal
organism, and that when the bacilli infect the blood-stream, temperature
rises ; when the lesions are closed, no escape of bacilli or their products
takes place, and the temperature is not affected.

Coming to the more definite indications of glanders, we have a long
list of separate symptoms, which may appear singly, or in numbers. No
one can be said to be always the pioneer—sometimes one, sometimes
another, ushers in the disease, and therefore the order in which they are
described is merely a matter of convenience.

Constitutional Disturbance, as evidenced by fever, loss of appetite,
and some quickening of circulatory and respiratory movements, usually
attends the onset of glanders. It may be temporary and be overlooked,
and it may not appear till the arrival of other symptoms. This is the
stage at which errors are often made, and a diagnosis of common cold or
catarrh may distract attention from the real mischief. Such an error is
easily made, and when no more definite symptom is visible we cannot
blame the practitioner. Any slight constitutional disturbance accompanied by a nasal discharge should be suspected, unless some definite
disease is recognised. When in doubt, the mallein test should be
applied.

Glandular Enlargements.   The most frequent glandular enlargement is that of the sub-maxillary lymphatic glands. As a rule, the gland
on only one side is affected, but in a few cases both are enlarged. A
very slight thickening is the first stage, and in some chronic cases nothing
more is noticeable for weeks. The gland may reach the size of half an
apple. It is hard, not painful, and very seldom suppurates. Usually it
is adherent to the jaw-bone and accompanied by little or no surrounding
œdema. The enlargement of gland may be the only symptom of
glanders, and may remain without complication for a long time. It may

be accompanied by an intermittent nasal discharge, which is noticeable during work, but ceases shortly after the horse has returned to his stable. The enlarged maxillary gland is very persistent, but it may entirely subside. In cases where a gland has once been enlarged and resumed its normal aspect, it may become a very prominent hard swelling in the short space of a day, or at most two, but is then always accompanied by some marked development of the disease—by acute generalisation of an old latent infection.

In Great Britain we have very few cases of glanders in entire horses. In countries where castration is not so general the testicles are often affected, showing swelling and pain on pressure. It should be remembered that tuberculosis may cause a similar condition. An undiagnosable lameness has occasionally been the first symptom noticed in a horse that later has developed glanders, and a post-mortem examination has disclosed specific disease in the inguinal, or in the brachial glands. Such cases are rare. When glanders was not so specially cared for as now—in old cases which had been temporarily cured (?) and had again developed, enlargement of the pre-pectoral glands was occasionally met with ; they could be felt in front of the border of the scapula. In cases of farcy with enormous swelling of a hind leg, the inguinal glands are usually affected.

Nasal Discharge is a very frequent symptom of glanders. In nearly all but the acute cases, the discharge is from one nostril. In acute cases, the discharge may be copious and distinctly purulent in appearance, but more often it is muco-purulent, of a dirty grey colour and a viscid nature. It may be streaked with blood. In chronic cases with a one-sided discharge, the matter is thinner, sticky, and less in quantity. It adheres to the edges of the nasal opening, and is often accompanied by some swelling and hardening of the skin covering the nares. The nasal discharge in glanders is not proportionate to the amount of ulceration of the nasal membrane—sometimes being slight when deep ulceration exists, and at other times copious with very few ulcerating lesions. The discharge may be intermittent and only seen after exercise or exertion. As a rule, no offensive smell accompanies the nasal discharge in glanders.

Nasal Nodules and Ulceration.   Very seldom is nasal ulceration seen in any other disease of horses but glanders.   It may occur: when it does, the ulcerating surface is raised and prominent, accompanied by very little discharge, and no constitutional symptoms are noticeable. Of course, all such cases should be tested with mallein.

Glanderous ulceration may exist high up on the septum, or on the turbinated bones, and cannot be seen during life.   When the ulceration is visible, we usually find it on the septum, or within the fold of mucous membrane which covers the anterior portion of the cartilage forming the alæ nasi.   White firm nodules are sometimes found on the nasal membrane, but they are not common.   They differ in size from that of a pin head to a small pea.   The most common lesion forming the first stage of ulceration is a small white vesicle which does not persist, but in about twenty-four hours breaks, leaving a red sore which forms a rapidly progressing ulcer.   *(Plate V.)*   This ulcer is round, with a dark red circumference, a depressed centre, and clean-cut raised border.   When near the entrance of the nose, the discharge from the ulcer often forms a soft scab over it, which is easily detached.   As a rule, more than one ulcerating spot makes its appearance, and when two or more are near they soon coalesce, forming an angry looking ulcerating patch.   In the worst cases the whole mucous membrane of the nasal passages may be one continuous ulcerating surface, and perforation of the septum has frequently been seen.   *(Plate IX.)*

Although the early ulcerations visible on the nasal membrane are rightly described as depressed ulcers with raised borders, those higher up the cavity, or which have existed for some days, are frequently prominent and almost fungous-looking objects.

Nasal Infiltration.   In some cases of glander—frsequently in the so-called "farcy" cases, we find no ulceration in the nasal cavity, but a swollen and discoloured membrane of a bluey-black colour.   The veins and lymphatics are distended and prominent, but the mucous membrane is unbroken. *(Plate XI.)*

This blue-black condition of the membrane is also seen in hard worked old horses—but to a less degree, and therefore is not to be accepted as an indication of infection without other symptoms.   It is, however, sufficiently suggestive to warrant a mallein test.

Snuffling and Snoring. As a result of nasal ulceration and œdema of the mucous membrane of the nose, the passage of air in respiration is obstructed; and we have snuffling and snoring as well marked symptoms of glanders. These conditions exist sometimes when very little can be detected by an examination of the nose in a living horse. The thickening and ulceration of membrane are too high up in the head to be visible, but their effects are most noticeable. Usually ulceration of the septum can be seen when these sounds are emitted by a glandered animal.

Roaring. When a horse has recently suffered from strangles or influenza, no surprise is felt at the emission of a "roaring" sound; but when a horse in regular work commences to "roar" suddenly, we are apt to suppose some traumatic cause to be in operation. This may be the very first noticeable symptom in the development of glanders. In every case of sudden roaring, so far as my experience goes, the horse has been the victim of latent glanders, and the roaring arises from ulceration of the larynx. Ulceration of the trachea may exist without a symptom to suggest its presence. Even ulceration of some parts of the larynx may cause no roaring, but when the lesions are on the anterior portions, on the vocal cords, the free border of the arytenoids, or on the epiglottis—roaring results. Such a symptom occurring in an infected stud is most suggestive, and wherever it happens without an apparent cause the mallein test should be resorted to. An error in diagnosis may induce a practitioner to resort to tracheotomy; this is attended by some danger to the operator.

Œdema of Limbs. In those cases of glanders which are first made evident by the appearance of lesions on the skin, swelling of the limbs is a common symptom. We may have a localised swelling on the arm or thigh, resembling a bruise. There is no history of injury and no sign of abrasion. The swelling is firm, irregular in shape, and slowly spreads. After a day or two, one or more small tumours or buds appear, and these rapidly suppurate.

A general œdema of the limbs often accompanies the development of glanders, as it does other debilitating conditions. "His legs are filled," say the stablemen. This slight dropsical effusion is most noticeable

below the knees and hocks, and may not be accompanied by any more
specific symptom. In many cases, however, small spots become prominent
and break, discharging a viscid fluid which mats together the hair, and,
running down the limb, leaves a track of dried brownish material, not
unlike varnish, firmly adherent to the hair.

In other cases œdema of the limbs is much more marked. As a
rule only one leg is affected, and the swelling is extensive, rapid and
painful. We have all the appearances of an acute lymphangitis, extending high up into the arm or thigh. Not until some other lesions appear
can we recognise this œdema as due to glanders. As a rule, we soon
have development of "buds" on the inside of the limbs, which give way
on the surface and allow of a discharge. One bud is followed by another
along the course of the lymphatic vessels, so that in time one finds a
series of lesions of different age—some unbroken, some suppurating,
some deep ulcers, and some healed or partially healed sores with a few
cicatrices.

The mallein test enables us to diagnose these cases in the earlier
stages, and the various developments of the "farcy buds" are themselves
quite indicative. It is necessary to remember that lymphangitis commences in the same manner; that epizoötic lymphangitis may closely
resemble the state I have tried to describe; and that another disease—
ulcerative lymphangitis—is sometimes only to be differentiated by failure
to react to mallein.

Tumours. There are two kinds of swellings seen in cutaneous
glanders—the well recognised farcy-bud and a larger tumour. These
larger tumours vary in size from one-and-a-half to three inches in
diameter; they show no tendency to suppurate, and are very persistent.
I have seen them remain for weeks, and if the horse be permitted to live,
they gradually decrease and finally disappear. If opened their contents
are found semi-gelatinous and of a straw colour, rarely purulent. Their
most common site is on the back and sides, less frequently over the
gluteal region. They are round, and as prominent as would be the third
of an orange laid on a flat surface. We seldom find more than one
or two at a time on any horse, and they are usually widely separated
from each other. It is worthy of note that these large tumours are never

accompanied by any enlargement of the lymphatic vessels in their neighbourhood, whereas the ordinary " bud " is seldom seen without its accompanying " cord."

The ordinary tumours, the farcy-buds, seldom exceed an inch in diameter. They may appear anywhere, but are most frequently seen on the face, neck, sides, and down the inner side of the limbs. The appearance of one is usually rapidly followed by others, arranged in a row and connected by a linear enlargement due to distension of lymphatic vessels, known as a " cord." These " buds " are first hard and prominent; they rapidly soften, the skin gives way, suppuration takes place, and an angry ulcerating surface with a depressed centre and thickened margin is left. The discharge is almost oily in character, and dries into adherent masses on the hair below the sore.

In a chain of farcy-buds every stage of the lesion may be seen—a partially healed bud marking the place first affected, then one just broken, then one softening, and two or three more, diminishing in size, which are still hard. On the fine skin of the face they seldom exceed half-an-inch in diameter, and when the ulceration stage is reached, they show very clearly the deep sunken condition with thickened margins, which is most characteristic of sores in glanders. *(Plate I.)*

Hard Swellings, irregular in shape and varying in size, are not uncommon in the early stage of cutaneous glanders. They appear on the limbs above the hocks and knees, on the sides, and on the sternum and abdomen. They vary in size, often reaching a measurement of 8 or 10 inches in length, and resemble a bruise rather than the enlargements of purpura.

Swelling of Joints. It is not common to find swollen joints in horses suffering from glanders, but in a few cases we have rapidly developed enlargements of knees and hocks—the latter joint presenting a well-marked " bog spavin." Specific inflammation of bursæ is also sometimes seen. I remember one case in the days when " farcy " was not doomed to slaughter, in which bog-spavins and wind-galls were very prominent, and caused some stiffness for a week or two. The horse afterwards worked for a year and these lesions entirely disappeared, but glanderous pleurisy ultimately killed him.

Pneumonia and Pleurisy. A horse suffering from latent glanders may, like other animals, be attacked by pneumonia or pleurisy, and these conditions then cause generalisation of the specific disease. Even after a post-mortem examination, it is not easy to say whether the lung symptoms and lesions are specific or only accidental complications.

In the donkey, experimental inoculation always causes pneumonia, and in most cases of acute glanders in the horse we have pneumonic complications.

There is, too, a specific glanderous pleurisy. It is not sudden in its onset, but develops gradually, and is accompanied by copious effusion into the chest. Signs of glanders may show themselves before the case proves fatal; but death may occur without the appearance of any specific symptom.

Although every visible case of glanders exhibits some of the symptoms I have noticed, few show them all.

TABLE VII.

SYMPTOMS SHOWN IN 1000 CASES OF GLANDERS OCCURRING IN LONDON BETWEEN APRIL AND NOVEMBER, 1901.

Symptoms.	Number of Horses.	Percentage.
Farcy, swellings, buds or ulcers, some verified by mallein test ...	414	41.4
Farcy and enlarged sub-maxillary glands	54	5.4
Nasal discharge, enlarged glands and farcy	82	8.2
Nasal discharge, ulcerated or infiltrated nasal membrane and enlarged glands	158	15.8
Nasal discharge, enlarged glands and mallein reaction	42	4.2
Nasal discharge, ulceration, enlarged glands and farcy	12	1.2
Nasal discharge and ulceration	27	2.7
Nasal discharge and emaciation	12	1.2
Nasal discharge and mallein reaction	17	1.7
Nasal ulceration and enlarged glands	5	.5
Enlarged glands	6	.6
Enlarged glands and mallein reaction	40	4.0
Mallein reaction only	119	11.9
Diseased lungs and other diseases giving symptoms of a suspicious nature	12	1.2

Table VII. is an analysis of a thousand cases seen by the veterinary inspectors of London some years ago, when the disease was prevalent and when more time was allowed for the natural development of symptoms. This year very few cases present such well-marked signs of glanders, because they are detected early, and because a comparatively small number escape disclosure by the mallein test before they show any outward symptoms of disease.

The first two groups of this table, numbering 468 horses, and the last four, numbering 177, are free from nasal discharge; so that 64 per cent. of the glandered horses slaughtered in London would not probably infect a water-trough or nosebag up to the day of their death. In 355 horses there was nasal discharge. Only 279 showed all the classical symptoms of glanders—nasal discharge, nasal ulceration, and enlargement of the sub-maxillary gland. Thirty years ago only these 27·9 per cent. would have been positively diagnosed as glandered.

Sub-acute glanders is the most common form of the disease seen in London. The temperature ranges from 102 to 104. The appetite is not lost, and the horse may remain at work without showing ill-effects, other than fatigue and bodily wasting. These symptoms are often accompanied by an enlarged sub-maxillary gland, and later by a nasal discharge and visible ulceration.

Acute glanders is the term applied to cases in which the disease is generalised and the blood-stream invaded by the bacilli. The temperature is 105 or higher, appetite is lost, respiration is rapid and accompanied by snuffling or roaring, the pulse is much accelerated, a nasal discharge is seen from both nostrils, often tinged with blood, and a cutaneous eruption or swelled legs may also appear. The horse dies in a few days from the septicæmia and pneumonia.

Chronic glanders is the form in which some symptoms, such as an enlarged gland and slight nasal discharge exist without much rise of temperature. These cases are now rare, but were common when compulsory slaughter was not enforced. They might develop gradually from a latent case, but more often followed a sub-acute attack which had subsided after rest and treatment, in a horse of extra strong constitution.

Symptoms abated for a time—but few horses survived many months, and any violent upset to the general system, such as a dose of physic, excessive work, or the supervention of any acute disease, ended in rapid generalisation and death. These horses in olden times were separated from the stud and worked together. In double harness the pole of the vehicle was painted black, so that those who knew might be warned off. White states that he has known chronic glandered horses to work for two years before being killed.

Chronic cases of the cutaneous form were formerly not infrequent. A horse with a thick leg and a few old scars resulting from an acute attack of farcy might work for weeks or months without much alteration. In cases favourably treated all the symptoms might disappear, but the rule was for the sub-maxillary gland to remain enlarged and hard. In time the marked limb suffered again from an acute lymphangitis. Finally the temperature rose, nasal symptoms appeared, and death followed.

Although we now ignore the separation of the disease into Farcy and Glanders, there was no doubt some excuse for the distinction in practice. Very few cases of glanders (nasal), ever recovered sufficiently to resume work, and fewer still worked more than three or four months after the clinical signs of disease had disappeared. It was not so with farcy. Many horses with cutaneous glanders showed only a small chain of buds on the face or body. These suppurated and healed. The horses resumed work and continued at work for months, some for years, before succumbing to a revival of the disease. A small proportion—perhaps 2 per cent.—worked for years and never exhibited another sign of the disease. I believe these rare cases were chiefly those in which inoculation through the skin was the method of infection, and that few, if any bacilli from the local primary sore reached the lungs to form secondary lesions.

Well marked cases of farcy sometimes show no pulmonary nodules at the autopsy, and frequently only two or three recent typical hæmorrhagic centres. The greater number, however, are found to have nodules in the lungs, of a form and structure which demonstrate that they have been in existence for months anterior to the cutaneous symptoms.

Farcy lesions are nearly always secondary to disease in the lungs, and result from the escape of bacilli from pulmonary nodules and their passage through lymph and blood vessels to the skin.

Like tuberculosis, glanders may remain as a local infection for an indefinite time, or even end in a spontaneous recovery. Like tuberculosis, local lesions of glanders may undergo some degenerative change which permits of the escape of active bacilli, and ends in generalised disease.

POST-MORTEM APPEARANCES.

There is only one post-mortem lesion that may be expected in every case of glanders, viz.: nodules in the lungs. On two or three occasions I have failed to find pulmonary nodules in horses which showed during life distinct symptoms of farcy, and I believe these few cases were due to primary infection of the skin, which directly produced cutaneous lesions, and, with sufficient time, would have affected the lungs. The large majority of cases of farcy do not arise in this way—they are secondary signs of a long established latent infection; this is demonstrated by the old lung lesions found on post-mortem examination.

Lung Lesions. No matter in what way the causal organism enters the body, it will find its way to the lungs and produce nodules, if the horse survives for a week or two after infection. The lung nodules persist, whilst the lesions caused at the point of entry may entirely disappear.

The pulmonary nodule is the most important of glanders lesions; it is also the most durable. Ulcers on the skin may heal and disappear; ulcers on the mucous membrane of the respiratory passages may heal and leave only small cicatrices; but the lung nodule remains. Everywhere on the outside of the body the tendency of a glanders lesion is to suppurate and ulcerate. In the lungs, the nodule containing active bacilli alters but slowly, and the changes taking place in it present little tendency to invade neighbouring tissues, or to set up a violent necrotic action. Since horses have been slaughtered solely on the reactions to mallein, lung lesions have been examined in an earlier stage, and more or less free from the complications which accompany the generalisation of the disease. Even under these conditions variations in the size, form and quality of the nodules are noticeable, due principally to the age of the lesions, but also to the resistance offered by the pulmonary tissue of the individual horse.

I need hardly warn professional observers of the difference in all lungs brought about by the method of death, and by the time which elapses before a post-mortem is made. A horse that dies of glanders and upon which a post-mortem is held some hours after shows a deeper colour of all the organs than one which is killed, and probably bled, just before the examination. The side upon which an animal lies after death always shows a darker colour than that which is uppermost.

There is a great variation in the appearance of lungs taken from glandered horses. Many pulmonary changes are found which have resulted from inflammatory attacks having no connection with glanders, which occurred perhaps months previously, and which have subsided so far as to show no symptoms of the disease during life. These attacks leave portions of the lungs altered in colour and density. Parasitic invasions also leave their mark, sometimes in the form of large cysts and sometimes as small hard calcareous particles. The small calcareous bodies which feel like shot under the pleura, when of parasitic origin are generally more uniform and more widely spread throughout both lungs than the glanders nodules. They are all about the same age and density. They are more easily enucleated from their capsule, and the enveloping border is more definitely marked off from the surrounding tissue than in the case of the typical glanders nodule. Another cause of pathological variety is the specific pneumonia or pleurisy accompanying generalised glanders; also the pulmonary inflammations which may accidentally or coincidently arise in horses already suffering from latent glanders, and which super-impose their lesions upon those of the specific disease. In a case of gangrenous pneumonia, latent glanders in the lungs is generalised with startling rapidity, and the complication may be overlooked unless care is exercised.

The Typical Glanders Nodule is a firm, round body varying in size from a pin-head to a horse-bean. It may sometimes be seen as a little eminence under the pleura, but is best found by passing the fingers with gentle pressure over the wet surface of the lung. If the lungs have been removed for some hours from the carcase and their surface allowed to become dry, nodules are not easily felt—they should be examined immediately after removal, or should be wetted before an attempt is made to detect nodules by touch. Nodules frequently exist and afford no evidence to the eye, whilst readily distinguished by touch.

The more recent nodules may often be recognised as dark circular spots visible through the pleura. (*Plate* II.) When felt with the finger, they yield the impression of firm round objects embedded in the lung. Dark spots upon the pleura are not uncommon in horses quite free from glanders, but they are superficial—not nodular.

The term miliary glanders is sometimes used to describe the small nodules found in the lungs. It suggests at once a comparison with the miliary lesion formed in tuberculosis, in which thousands of small tubercles are distributed evenly all through the lung. Such a condition is seldom found in glanders, although nodules may exist throughout one or both lungs.

The Glanders Nodules are found irregularly here and there, chiefly on the upper surface of the lungs. As a rule more in one lung than the other. They often differ in age, some so old as to have become gritty, some caseous, and some merely dark hæmorrhagic centres.

Continental observers have described as the earliest stage of lung lesion due to the lodgment of the Bacillus mallei, a yellow semi-transparent speck about the size of a pin's-head. I confess I have not yet recognised this condition. The earliest change I am conversant with is a dark hæmorrhagic sphere, not very clearly defined from the surrounding lung tissue at its circumference, especially when exposed by a deep cut into the lungs. (*Plate* II.) How long this condition remains I do not know, but from a few cases in which the period of infection was known, I estimate such nodules to have been in existence for about a month or six weeks. The next stage is for this dark spot, when incised, to present a centre of a yellowish grey colour, which, in course of time, increases in size and becomes lighter in colour. (*Plate* III.) As the light coloured centre increases in size, the surrounding dark zone contracts, and becomes more distinctly defined from the surrounding lung. This change goes on until the whole nodule consists of a caseous grey mass varying in size from a pin's head to a pea. *(Plate* III.) The caseous nodules, if the horse lives, undergo a further development; they become gritty from calcareous alteration, and in some of the very oldest lesions we have a hard, solid, round body, not unlike a coated pill, which may be enucleated from its surrounding capsule. The fact of nodules of varying age existing together in a lung is not due to various dates of infection, but to the more or less constant escape of bacilli from the earlier nodules. These bacilli become lodged and form fresh nodules, and so we have from one infection an increase of nodules which may continue for years. There are often very few nodules in a lung, but no one should say there are none until he has not only felt every part of the organ through the uncut pleura, but sliced the lungs and examined each section with fingers and eyes.

When making deep incisions into a lung in search of glanders lesions, it should be remembered that the round nodule may slip aside from the knife, and then does not disclose the characteristic light coloured centre. It appears as a dark round prominence on the cut surface, and should be carefully divided so as to display its centre.

The deep incisions often disclose small abscesses; when these are about the size of a millet seed, and their contents better described as caseous than purulent, they are probably glanders lesions.

Every stage of the nodule may be found deep in the lung tissue, as just under the pleura, but they are less easily detected owing to the colour of the surrounding tissues, and to the hæmorrhage following the incision.

In some of the older cases, very few dark coloured nodules are found, but the incised surface shows numbers of small grey caseous masses, about the size of a small mustard seed, without any hæmorrhagic zone surrounding them.

So far I have attempted to describe a typical glanders lesion, but there are others not so well defined. There is a nodule or small tumour, varying in size from a hazel-nut to a walnut, which is easily seen as a prominent object under the pleura—this membrane being opaque and thickened over it. When cut into, the nodule is of irregular form and partly caseous. The section is not like that of the typical nodule having a well defined centre. It appears to have penetrated into the lung substance—a sort of interstitial infiltration, so that portions of lung tissue intersect the nodule, especially at its circumference. *(Plate* III.*)* Sometimes these large nodules show, when cut into, three or four separate caseous specks, or each may be a distinct abscess.

Pneumonia is always present in acute cases, and the whole lung is dark and congested. In some places softening has occurred and small abscesses are found, but cavities such as occur in tuberculosis are rare in glanders. Large dark coloured masses, the size of an orange, are sometimes seen, which, when cut into, show one or more small abscesses. Similar lesions are seen in cases of pneumonia not accompanied by glanders—and, therefore, they cannot be accepted by themselves as evidence of the specific disease. When glanders nodules happen to be situated in a portion of inflamed lung they very rapidly develop, forming small abscesses containing pus of a firmer and more caseous quality than that due to other pulmonary inflammations.

Pleurisy is not uncommon, and may be specific, or co-incidental with latent glanders. A firm layer of tough adherent lymph covers the pleura, and effectually prevents the detection of nodules by the hand. Unless a lung is well filled with nodules, the changes resulting from pleurisy may render it very difficult to decide whether pulmonary glanders is present or not.

Fibroid Changes in the lungs as specific glanders lesions are not often seen. Occasionally, a swelling the size of a small apple is met with, which on being cut into is found firm, hard, and light coloured. Probably such morbid changes have no relation to the glanders lesions also present. The extensive fibroid change which is described as due to old standing tuberculosis is very rare in glanders. Only once have I seen a lung, the borders and apex of which were so firm and hard that it could hardly be cut with a knife. That case I know was infected for nine years; although it showed no clinical sign of disease, except for the first three months of that time.

The Spleen. Next in frequency to the lungs, nodules are found in the spleen. They may be detected by the fingers as small, firm bodies under the capsule. They are generally rendered very noticeable by a red or reddish stain of the capsule covering them. *(Plate* IV.*)* When cut into, they resemble the pulmonary nodule, but are seldom seen in the hæmorrhagic stage—if that is ever the primary state of a splenic nodule. The grey mass which they usually present when incised is firmer and less caseous than the similar lesion of the lung.

The Liver is not often the seat of glanders nodules, but they are occasionally found in this organ. They present the form of a whitey-grey spot on the capsule.

The Kidney is very rarely the site of glanders lesions, and when they are found their nature can only be determined by biological experiment.

The Intestines are said to disclose glanders ulceration to careful observation. I have never seen such lesions. They would be most likely to exist very shortly after ingestion of active bacilli, or in a very acute case of generalised glanders in which the virus from ulcerated respiratory passages passed into the pharynx and then through the stomach.

Lesions of the Respiratory Passages.

The lesions found on the mucous membrane lining the respiratory passages are vesicles, nodules, ulcers, infiltrations and cicatrices. These, except perhaps the infiltrations, are always secondary lesions, caused by the escape of bacilli from nodules in the lungs. I have never seen ulceration of nasal or tracheal mucous membrane without finding nodules in the lungs of an age much greater than the ulcerations.

The Vesicle is a small circular blister, almost transparent. In a few hours the upper part of the raised membrane gives way, disclosing a red sore which rapidly proceeds to ulcerate. These vesicles may be solitary, but more often are found in clusters. *(Plate* V.*)* As each breaks down and forms a sore they coalesce, and thus we have the rapid appearance of extensive ulcerated patches so noticeable in the more acute cases of glanders.

Nodules may occur on the septum, larynx and trachea, but are not common in these situations in the horse. They are small, white, firm bodies about the size of a small pea, or less. They are more persistent than the vesicle, but ultimately break down, forming a sore which rapidly ulcerates.

Ulceration. This is the most marked lesion of glanders. It is found in all clinically developed cases either on the skin, or on the respiratory mucous membrane. As a rule the ulcers are distinct and separate, but frequently we find them coalescing to form a large continuous ulcerated surface, and I have seen cases in which the whole of the nasal mucous membrane was affected, as well as most of that covering the larynx and trachea. The turbinated bones and the large sinuses of the head are often affected, in addition to the nasal cavity. *(Plate X.)* Even the guttural pouches and Eustachian tube have been found ulcerated.

Tracheal Ulceration presents two very different forms, one—the more common—in which large solitary ulcers are found quite apart from each other. They are not below the surface of the surrounding tissue, but prominent and raised, dark in colour, and bathed in pus. *(Plate VI.)* The other form resembles a series of red streaks running always vertically to the direction of the trachea. They are not solitary, but are found in great numbers, often extending over the whole length of the mucous membrane. They may be well described as narrow slits through which protrudes a bright red granulation. *(Plate VII.)*

Laryngeal Ulceration usually takes the form of isolated ulcers varying in size up to that of a sixpence. They are found on the epiglottis, on the vocal cords, and on the border of the arytenoids, as well as on other parts of the laryngeal membrane. In a few cases the whole larynx presents one continuous ulcerated surface. *(Plate VIII.)*

Nasal Ulceration is usually found in long patches on the septum nasi, and a similar form is seen on the membrane covering the turbinated bones. *(Plate X.)* In some cases it is located high up on the septum, in others we find only one, or perhaps two small ulcers at the lower end of the cartilage, which are visible during life.

In some chronic cases when nasal ulceration has been continued for a long time, we may have perforation right through the septum, and this condition is found more often at the lower extremity of the septum than at the upper. *(Plate IX.)*

The usual colour of the ulcerating surface on membrane lining the respiratory passages is an angry red, covered by a blood-stained muco-purulent secretion. In a few cases we find a pale yellowish-grey surface covered with a viscid translucent mucus. This condition is the healing stage of the ulcerative process.

Cicatrices are found in the trachea, larynx and nose. In the two first positions they are generally small, but on the nasal membrane covering the septum they may be extensive. Their usual size is about that of a shilling or less. They are irregularly stellate in form, smooth, and white. In conjunction with a cicatrix, it is not uncommon to find neighbouring lesions in a healing stage—instead of the angry coloured ulcerations we see straw coloured masses of granulation tissue. This is well shown in *Plate* XII.

Now-a-days, when cases of glanders are closely looked after in London and slaughtered as soon as detected, these cicatrices are becoming very rare. A stellate cicatrix on the septum of a horse so seldom results from anything but a healed glanders ulcer, that its presence should suggest an immediate test with mallein.

Infiltration. In glanders the nasal septum is often the seat of thickening and discoloration with no ulceration. Sometimes the whole substance of the membrane is a bluey-black colour, raised and thickened by effusion beneath it. When the discolouration is only partial the rest of the membrane is prominently marked by distended small veins. *(Plate* XI.) I have found portions of the membrane covering the septum almost black, and raised quite half-an-inch by effusion under it. On cutting through the membrane a dark sanguineous mass was found, firmer than clotted blood—almost the consistency of a soft tumour. I ought to add that in some cases of farcy I have seen this infiltration accompanied by very few pulmonary nodules, and I am not sure that, like the ulcerations, it is always due to the escape of bacilli from the lungs. So frequently in cases of farcy do I find the membrane covering the septum infiltrated but not ulcerated, that I have formed the opinion that the nasal membranes are specially selected parts for the attacks of glanders, just as the feet and buccal membranes are for foot-and-mouth disease in the ox. The frequency of nasal ulceration is easily accounted for by the passage upwards from the lungs of glanders bacilli. But nasal infiltration is found accompanying cutaneous glanders, even in cases where no pulmonary nodules can be detected.

Glandular Lesions. Among the symptoms of glanders I mentioned enlarged glands. Post-mortem they can be more thoroughly studied than during life, because available both before and after section. The submaxillary gland is often enlarged; and although it seldom forms an abscess such as occurs in strangles, we may, on section, find small collections of caseous pus. The more common changes in the gland are softening and distension of the lobules by effusion within them, a yellowish exudate in the connective tissue around them, and one or more grey spots in the lobule when incised. Lymphatic lobules vary in colour in healthy horses, they are yellowish white, reddish, or sometimes black, but whatever the colour it is uniform throughout. Whitey-grey centres in the lobules are the lesions of glanders. (*Plate* XIII.) The bronchial and thoracic lymphatic glands are often the seat of lesions in glanders, but not so often as when the lungs are affected by tuberculosis. (*Plate* XIV.) The mesenteric glands are seldom the seat of any specific lesion in cases of natural infection. Glanders, experimentally produced by ingestion of pure cultures, has caused mesenteric lesions, but it must be remembered that the culture used contained probably a hundred times as many active bacilli as would be found in a similar quantity of the most virulent natural infective material.

Muscular Lesions are found in man in the form of large intramuscular abscesses. I have never seen such changes in the horse, nor do I recognise any other muscular lesion in this animal.

Joint Lesions. Not often does glanders in horses cause any change in joints which can be detected after death. I have seen hocks and knees during life show synovial distension without any signs of acute pain. In man, joints frequently are enlarged and painful in acute glanders, and are sometimes the seat of purulent synovitis. Such a condition in the horse, I believe, is unknown.

Cutaneous Lesions are tumours, abscesses, ulcers, and inflamed lymphatics vessels. The larger tumours I described in the section on Symptoms. The smaller—known as farcy-buds, occur singly or in chains. Appearing first as small, round, hard tumours, they soon soften, the top gives way allowing the escape of a dirty, blood-stained pus or of an oily fluid, and the base remains, showing an angry red surface with little tendency to heal. The lymphatic vessels around this "bud" become inflamed and swollen, along their course other buds form, and so we have the familiar chain of buds connected by enlarged lymph vessels—the so-called "cords." (*Plate* I.)   When the cutaneous form of glanders is permitted to exist, a very large area may soon be covered with "buds," ulcers, and "cords." In some chronic cases a bud or two make their appearance, enlarge slowly, and then as slowly decrease and disappear. When the skin is removed from a part showing cutaneous lesions, a condition is often revealed quite disproportionate to the mild changes seen on the surface during life. The lymphatic vessels have become purulent sinuses; subcutaneous abscesses, sometimes the size of a man's hand, are found, and a large area may be infiltrated with straw-coloured effusion.

All these different lesions may be found in one case, but not often. Sometimes we find only one or two, sometimes a number, but the association of lesions apparently follows no rule, and the results of a post-mortem examination can never be anticipated with any certainty. The following table shows how glanders lesions were actually grouped in 1,000 cases examined by the Veterinary Inspectors of the London County Council. Probably the table gives a truer idea of the natural condition of the disease than we should obtain now by similar statistics, for in 1908 mallein and slaughter have not left the old, undeveloped cases such as were frequent in 1901.

Of the 1000 cases, 462 presented nodules in the lungs as the only internal lesions. The nasal membrane was ulcerated in 378 horses, the larynx in 179, and the trachea in 201.

In the 46 horses whose lungs contained very few nodules, no lesion of the membrane was found. Probably nearly all these were free from clinical symptoms and were slaughtered on a mallein reaction only. Some might have been cases of cutaneous glanders. It is worthy of note that out of 1000 cases, 954 showed distinct nodular lesions in the lungs.

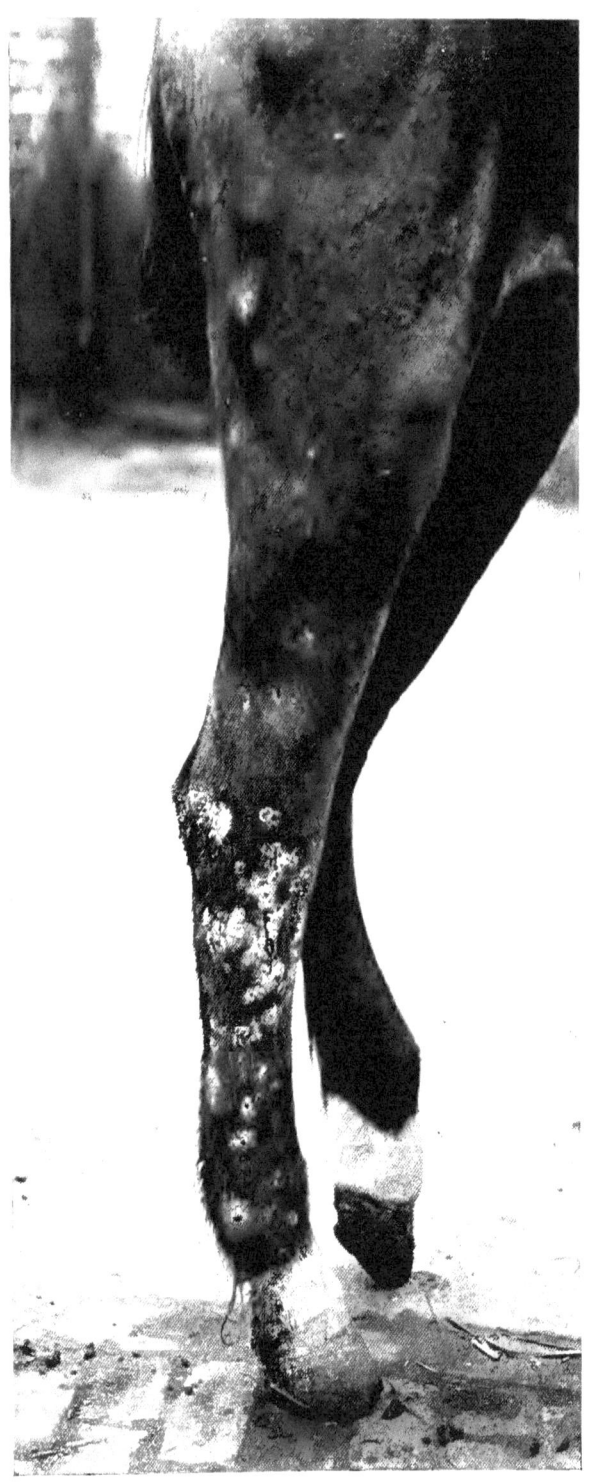

Cutaneous Glanders (Farcy) on a hind limb, showing ulcerating and some partially healed sores. Unbroken "buds" on the thigh. (Cutaneous Lesions, p. 50.)

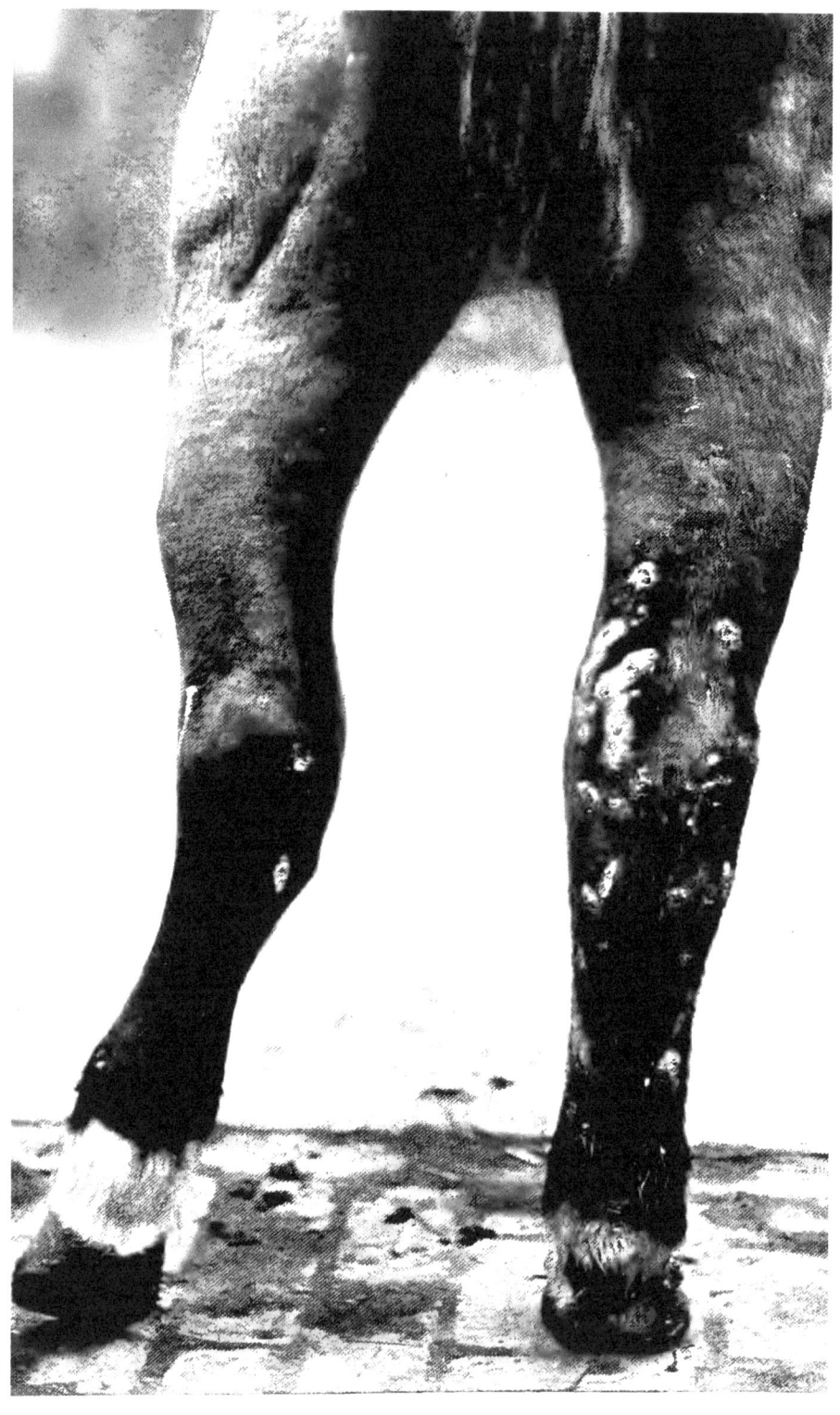

Back view of same horse. A "bud" on right thigh is very prominent. Small suppurating sore on left hock. (Cutaneous Lesions, p. 50.)

TABLE VIII.

LESIONS SHOWN IN 1000 POST-MORTEM EXAMINATIONS OF GLANDERED
HORSES IN LONDON BETWEEN APRIL AND NOVEMBER, 1901.

	Lesions.	No. of Horses.
Group I	Lungs fairly full of glanders nodules	295
	,, Nasal membrane ulcerated	101
	,, Nasal membrane infiltrated	95
	,, Trachea ulcerated	19
	,, Larynx and trachea ulcerated	16
	,, Nasal membrane and larynx ulcerated ...	9
Group II	Lungs full of glanders nodules	121
	,, Nasal membrane ulcerated	128
	,, Nasal membrane, larynx and trachea ulcerated	124
	,, Larynx and trachea ulcerated	26
	,, Nasal membrane and trachea ulcerated ...	16
	,, Larynx ulcerated	4
Group III	Lungs contained few glanders nodules	46

The development of glanders lesions is most irregular in cases of natural infection. Some horses that we know have been long infected show very few lesions on a post-mortem examination. Others with a short period of infection are found after death to present extensive morbid changes. Doubtless one cause of this variation is the dose of bacilli received at the time of infection. One horse may be infected by one dose of virus contained in one feed or one pail of contaminated water. Another may for many days be stabled alongside an infected animal, and thus ingest a number of small but repeated doses. Then there is the state of the horse to remember—his individual resisting power or his susceptibility. One may be infected and live a year or more without a clinical sign of infection showing. Another dies of generalised lesions in a few weeks.

It is therefore almost impossible to form an opinion, even after a post-mortem examination, on the question of the duration of the disease. In only a few cases where an autopsy is possible do we know the exact date of infection, and unless this is known it is impossible to arrive at a sound basis for any definite conclusions. Without sufficient data, but with a number of cases in view in which a post-mortem has been obtained and in which the time of infection has been fixed to a week or two, I have ventured to form some opinions. When the lung lesions are only hæmorrhagic nodules they are not more than a month old. When nodules are caseous they may be six months, and when calcareous probably twelve months old. When nodules of all stages exist, I fix the duration by the state of the oldest. In cases where acute glanders has existed for some days, or in which infected horses have been continuously overworked or underfed, I think it probable that my estimates of duration would be useless, and that the changes in the lungs would be much more rapid up to the caseous stage. A similar difficulty occurs in fixing the age of ulcerating lesions. In some horses extensive changes occur in a day or two, in others ulceration goes on for a week or two, and then is limited to patches.

In the majority of cases it is very rash to express an opinion as to the age of glanders lesions.

Very little assistance is given the clinical observer by the experiments of pathologists, who use pure cultures as infecting media. I suppose that a fluid drachm of a pure culture, or a scraping from a growth on potato, might contain as many active bacilli as half-a-pint of any natural infective discharge. The result is that these artificial infections act much more rapidly and with tenfold more violence than any natural infective material.

Nocard, Schütz, and M'Fadyean have experimentally produced glanders by causing horses to swallow pure cultures of the bacillus. In some of Nocard's cases, clinical symptoms were evident on the eighth day, and mallein gave a reaction on the seventh. Horses killed 15 days after infection were found by Nocard to have their lungs full of nodules in all stages. Horses killed three months after infection had their lungs literally crammed with nodules—fibrous, calcareous and caseous.

Schütz made post-mortem examinations on the 14th, 15th, and 25th days after infection, and found nodules in the lungs. He also found what Nocard did not describe—enlarged mesenteric glands, nodules in the spleen and intestines, enlarged abdominal lymphatic glands, and distended chyle vessels. Nocard found calcareous nodules in a case only three months after infection. These findings are certainly not in accordance with the lesions seen in natural infections. I think I may say positively that I have never seen calcareous changes in lesions less than six months old.

M'Fadyean infected four ponies by administering scrapings from potato cultures in such a manner as to avoid any method of infection save that of ingestion. In each case glanders nodules were found in the lungs, but only in one were distinct lesions found in the mesenteric glands. From the December number, 1907, of *The Journal of Comparative Pathology and Therapeutics* I take the following extracts from Sir John M'Fadyean's Harben Lectures.

Case I. Post-mortem made on eighth day after infection. " The whole of the mesenteric glands were congested and considerably enlarged, though none was as large as a pigeon's egg. The lymphatic glands belonging to the double colon were also enlarged, the largest being about the size of a garden bean, and small opaque necrotic-looking areas were present in many of these. . . . One nodule was found in the spleen. . . .

In the small intestine, under the mucous membrane there were two slightly projecting nodules, the larger about the size of a vetch pea. . . .

The lungs contained some hundreds of nodules with the ordinary appearance of glanders nodules. They varied in size between a filbert and a barley grain. On section the nodules showed a central grey or dirty-white opaque area and a peripheral congested or hæmorrhagic zone. No lesions were visible in the thoracic lymphatic glands.

Numerous small nodules were present under the mucous membrane of the nose, both on the septum nasi and the turbinated bones."

Case II. Post-mortem made on the fifteenth day after infection. " Nothing abnormal in any of the abdominal lymphatic glands. The stomach and intestines, both large and small, showed no abnormality. The spleen was normal in size, but a pea-sized nodule was present under the capsule. The lungs contained five nodules about the size of a vetch pea. No other lesions were discovered anywhere."

Case III. Post-mortem on twentieth day. " The whole of the mesenteric glands were quite normal. . . . The spleen was normal save for one typical glanders nodule. . . . The lungs contained a dozen or more typical glanders nodules.

Case IV. Post-mortem on fourteenth day after infection. "No glanders lesions were found in the abdominal cavity, although nodules were present in the lungs."

These cases afford positive evidence that infection by ingestion of glanderous material may produce nodules in the lungs in from eight to twenty days, and cause no macroscopic lesion in the abdominal organs, through which the bacilli must have passed. In Case I, mesenteric and intestinal lesions were caused, and probably were noticeable owing to the short time which elapsed between infection and the post-mortem examination.

Incidentally another fact was disclosed in these experiments—that each case except the first reacted to an injection of mallein on the thirteenth day after infection.

There is just one more point I must refer to before leaving the pulmonary lesions. The existing Order provides that in case of dispute between an Inspector and the Veterinary Surgeon representing the owner, as to the presence of disease, the lungs or other necessary parts shall be sent to the Board of Agriculture—whose decision is final. We all know that cases occur in which Mallein gives a good reaction, but no pulmonary lesions are discovered. It is probable that in these rare cases some undiscovered lesions really exist. Probably the Board would fail to find any indication of glanders in such cases, even by culture experiments. But there are cases in which pulmonary nodules may be found that are not due to glanders; and so the regulation of the Board is just, and the provision for a final judgment, after scientific tests, is fair to everybody. Of course, the absence of lung nodules would not be evidence of freedom from disease if cutaneous symptoms existed, and these "farcy" lesions would have to be forwarded before a decision could be given.

DIAGNOSIS.

When a horse presents a nasal discharge, nasal ulceration, and an enlarged submaxillary gland, diagnosis is easy. A swollen leg and a typical chain of farcy "buds" is another form of the disease about which no doubt need exist. But there are many cases of glanders in which the symptoms are not well marked, and there are some other diseases which at times closely resemble glanders. There are also cases in which the symptoms of glanders may be masked by the morbid changes due to other maladies.

An Enlarged Submaxillary Gland may exist for some time before any other sign is apparent. This symptom may also arise from disease of teeth or sinuses, but usually is then accompanied by a unilateral nasal discharge with an offensive smell. An enlarged gland may be due to Melanosis, which only occurs in grey horses, and is attended by no nasal discharge, but often by tumours in other parts of the body. Another rare cause of enlarged submaxillary gland is tuberculosis. In some unusual cases of glanders the submaxillary gland suppurates, and the condition may be mistaken for strangles, but the slow development of these cases should cause their true nature to be suspected. An injection of mallein assists diagnosis, and should be resorted to at once on the appearance of glandular enlargement.

Strangles, Catarrh and Influenza very often show a purulent nasal discharge which has been confidently credited as peculiar to those diseases. It is not sufficient to observe the character of the discharge. Many cases of glanders commence with a purulent or semi-purulent discharge not distinguishable from that of other diseases. Some cases of latent glanders are wakened into activity by an attack of catarrhal fever. These are the cases which led to the error of supposing that "influenza turned to glanders." In young horses a nasal discharge may usually be accepted as innocent, but from an old horse should be treated with care. Newly purchased horses from a town stud should always be suspected if they exhibit a nasal discharge, and the mallein test should be applied.

Nasal Ulceration is almost diagnostic of glanders, but slaughter should not be adopted until mallein has been used, unless the character of the ulceration or other symptoms are such as to leave no doubt.

Nettle Rash has been mistaken for cutaneous glanders. Although the swellings at first somewhat resemble farcy buds, their sudden appearance, their general prevalence over the body, and their tendency to coalesce, should be sufficient to found a diagnosis upon. The nettle-rash lumps disappear as rapidly as they make their appearance. Only once have I seen a case of acute glanders with the skin covered with lumps about the size of walnuts—they were all about one size, and discrete. The horse was killed on other symptoms, and I considered the case one in which the two diseases co-existed.

Purpura hæmorrhagica has often been mistaken for glanders. When the head is badly affected, we find swollen nostrils, a blood-stained septum, and a sanguineous discharge from the nose. These conditions may mask a case of latent glanders which has been generalised by the purpura. It is extremely difficult to open the swollen nostril in these horses sufficiently to see the septum. The swelling of the limbs may be mistaken for farcy of the legs, but as a rule farcy appears only in one leg, whereas the swellings of purpura are in two, or in all four, and in size and position bi-latterally symmetrical. At the commencement of a case of purpura, dark spots upon the septum nasi may suggest the use of mallein. The temperature is always raised—often high, so is useless as a reaction symptom. In almost every case of purpura, swelling at the point of injection is considerable, but as it rises in twenty-four hours, so it disappears in the next twenty-four, and its rapid subsidence indicates freedom from glanders.

Laryngeal Disease may cause roaring in horses, and occasionally this symptom is the first to show itself in glanders. When roaring comes on suddenly, suspicion should be aroused, and the fact of its disappearance and recurrence should not permit a diagnosis of non-specific disease. The sudden access of roaring without any clear cause should be followed by an injection of mallein, especially in town horses or those newly purchased.

Ulcerative Lymphangitis. There is a form of lymphangitis which may be mistaken for cutaneous glanders of the limb. In addition to the general dropsical enlargement of the limb, we have a sub-cutaneous collection of pus, causing sloughing of a comparatively large portion of skin inside the thigh. Then the lymphatic vessels become enlarged and suppurate, and smaller abscesses form around and below the original wound. These small abscesses are often very similar in appearance to farcy buds, but the larger sloughs almost differentiate the two diseases. An injection of mallein affords most reliable aid to diagnosis.

Horse Pox. Some cases of horse-pox very closely resemble glanders on a superficial examination. They may have as symptoms a nasal discharge, enlarged maxillary glands, and small ulcers on the fine skin of the nose and lips. But there are other lesions, not found in glanders, viz.: vesicles, which soon form ulcers, on the mucous membrane of the lips. These ulcers are not like the malignant ulcers of glanders, they are not so deep, show no tendency to spread and soon heal.

What is called *Stomatitis pustulosa contagiosa* is, I believe, only horse-pox (Equine Variola), under another name. When stomatitis happens to accompany lesions in the heel and back of the fetlock, no one disputes that the case is one of variola, especially if depilation follows, and the legs lose most of their hair. Stomatitis confined to the lips is communicable to man, and in two or three cases I have seen, the human lesion from accidental inoculation was typically variolous.

Botriomycosis. Not often can this disease be mistaken for glanders. In one case in which some similarity existed, there were two tumours on the inside of the thigh of the horse—one the size of a walnut, the other as large as a Tangerine orange. There was also an irregular, hard swelling on the antero-inferior aspect of the sternum. The tumours had been present for some weeks and had suppurated. The swelling on the breast had just appeared, and this led to doubt of the nature of the case. Mallein was injected and gave no reaction. Afterwards Sir John M'Fadyean cleared up the mystery by discovering the botriomyces.

Epizootic Lymphangitis is now a non-existent disease in Great Britain, but in some countries it is prevalent. There are cases of the disease which only the most experienced practitioners can distinguish from the cutaneous forms of glanders. The mallein test should be resorted to at once, and the negative results should be followed by a microscopic examination of the pus from the sores so as to obtain a positive diagnosis. This is reached by the discovery of the lemon-shaped cells of the causal organism in epizootic lymphangitis.

In the second edition of Captain W. A. Pallin's book on "Epizootic Lymphangitis," is a very carefully arranged differential diagnosis of the disease from glanders which I am permitted to quote :

(1) Healthy appearance of the animal generally, emaciation and unthriftyness being only present in very advanced cases in which the disease tends to become generalised.

(2) Almost invariable absence of fever.

(3) Unimpaired appetite.

(4) Characteristic appearance of the ulcers and sores which have an inclination to granulate and, with energetic treatment, to heal.

(5) The whitish colour and thick creamy consistency of the pus.

(6) The benign and curable character of the disease.

(7) Non-reaction to mallein.

(8) Inconstancy of sub-maxillary glandular enlargement, even in cases where the nasal mucous membranes are the seat of the disease.

(9) In the nasal variety, the ulcerations in glanders are generally more extensive, and, in most cases, spread from above downwards, whereas in this disease, the ulcerations are generally less extensive, and are more frequently found in the lower third of the nasal chambers.

(10) The invariable presence of the cryptococcus in the pus and tissues.

Epizootic lymphangitis in an Indian country-bred horse, infection having taken place during the time that the animal was under treatment for strangles for some weeks previously. The case was cured, and the lesions seen now, developed later ; all the tissues in the submaxillary space were more or less affected, multiple pustules formed, and the disease spread round the jaw, across the face, Stenson's duct also becoming the seat of an abscess. From a photograph taken in India. Diagnosis verified by microscopical examination and mallein testing.

From Pallin's "Epizootic Lymphangitis." By permission.

Aids to Diagnosis. There are many methods suggested for verifying a diagnosis of glanders. The microscope may be used to show the bacilli in the pus or juices of a suspected lesion. If a man is expert in using the microscope and in staining preparations, he may identify the organism, but in the majority of cases a practitioner would be well advised to leave this method to the trained bacteriologist.

The Agglutination test is another means of assisting diagnosis which is only useful in the hands of an expert. I am indebted to Mr. Leslie Sheather, Pathological Assistant to Sir John M'Fadyean, for the following note:

" The Agglutination Test for the diagnosis of glanders depends upon the fact that the serum of an animal that is the subject of the disease contains some specific body which causes the agglutination, or clumping together of glanders bacilli in liquid media. It appears to be of no consequence whether the bacilli be alive or dead. Normal serum possesses this power of agglutinating organisms and foreign cells to some extent, but in the case of a specific infection the power is very greatly increased.

" Briefly stated, the method of applying the test is as follows:—To a suspension of glanders bacilli in normal saline solution ($\frac{3}{4}$% sod. chlor.) is added serum taken from the animal that is the subject of the test, in varying proportions, *e.g.*, 1 part of serum in 200, 400, 600, 800 and 1000, of the suspension. These mixtures are then incubated at 37°C. for 24 hours, or at the most 72 hours. During this period the agglutination takes place, the bacilli congregating into clumps and finally settling to the bottom, leaving the liquid, which was previously uniformly hazy on account of the suspended bacilli, clear. It is upon the extent to which this takes place that an opinion is formed. If no agglutination has taken place in the dilutions from 400 to 1000 one is entitled to say that the serum used was taken from an animal free from glanders.

" If on the other hand agglutination has taken place in all the dilutions the animal from which the serum was taken may be declared glandered. Intermediate results are sometimes somewhat difficult of interpretation. It is always advisable to carry out the test simultaneously with serum taken from an animal known to be free from glanders as a control."

Inoculation of other animals, such as horses, asses or guinea-pigs may also be adopted, but it is expensive and requires time for development. Inoculation into a susceptible animal gives positive demonstration if active bacilli are present in the material used for injection. The discharges from any visible lesion are, however, mostly contaminated by mixed organisms, and sometimes wanting in active glanders bacilli. Inoculation of pus from the nose into the larger animals has often failed to give a definite result; and even separate nodules from one pair of glandered lungs, which appeared morphologically alike, have given some negative and some positive results when singly inoculated into guinea-pigs.

Cultivations of the bacilli are not easily carried out unless a tolerably pure material can be obtained. The discharge from the nose, or from an ulcer on the skin, contains so many other organisms that it is useless for culture purposes. When an unopened farcy bud exists, material can be obtained by incision which, in skilled hands, may afford good results from cultivation on sterilized potato.

All these aids to diagnosis are of use in their degree, but they can only be carried out by a bacteriologist in a laboratory; the general practitioner will find injection of mallein quite as trustworthy, much simpler, and more prompt in its indications.

MALLEIN.

Mallein was discovered in 1891 by Kalning and Helman, two Russian veterinarians. It is obtained by growing the Bacillus mallei for some weeks in a suitable medium and at a definite temperature. The resulting virulent culture is then heated in an autoclave, to kill all the organisms, and filtered through a porcelain filter to remove the dead bacilli. To the material thus obtained is added glycerine and a solution of carbolic acid.

Mallein so prepared is a transparent fluid of a pale yellowish brown colour. If injected under the skin of a healthy horse in small doses it produces no symptoms, save, perhaps, a swelling the size of half a walnut at the spot of injection. This swelling, which soon disappears, may be due to a dirty skin or a dirty needle, to mallein which has been allowed to become dirty, or even to too large and blunt a needle. When injected into a horse infected with glanders two effects result: a rise of the general temperature and a swelling at the seat of injection—which together constitute a specific reaction. This double reaction renders mallein more useful than tuberculin as a diagnostic agent, because in many cases of suspected glanders and tuberculosis an abnormally high temperature is present. The elevated temperature in the tuberculosis case renders tuberculin useless, but with a high temperature in glanders, we may still obtain some indication from the presence or absence of a local swelling. It is inadvisable to use either agent where the temperature is abnormal, but we may have to wait days for the temperature to reach the normal, and when diagnosis is urgent, mallein may be employed with hope of some guidance.

Mallein is injected under the skin in doses of twenty drops or less from a hypodermic syringe. Any part of the skin may be selected, but the best is the side of the neck, about half-way from the ear to the shoulder. Injection over the shoulder or ribs results in a needlessly painful swelling. Injection into the skin of a leg is followed by great lameness if a reaction takes place, and injection into the loose skin in front of the stifle causes a swelling, easily felt but not very visible. The neck as the site for injection has other points in its favour—the skin is easily lifted into a fold, the operator is in a good position if the horse is bad tempered, and the swelling of a reaction is well thrown up by the firm tissues underneath.

Most of the needles supplied with veterinary hypodermic syringes are too long and too thick. The finer the needle the more easily is it inserted and the less the horse resents it. There are two forms of junction between needle and syringe—the screw and the plug. The screw is the more objectionable, as the needle can only be used with the syringe attached, and when the horse is fidgetty or spiteful, the operator may have his choice between leaving the syringe hanging from the neck by the needle, or keeping his hold and being injured. The detached needle is easily inserted and remains in place if it has to be left, whilst the syringe with the plug junction is used with the greatest facility.

There are certain precautions which should be observed in the application of a mallein test. The first is to take the temperature of the animal before an injection is made. In a working stud of fifty horses, it is quite usual to find a horse, apparently well, with a temperature of 104, and as this may be the commencement of an illness which would lead to even a higher temperature, that animal is left over for a further test. When the injection is made without taking the temperatures, such cases are only discovered when the reaction is looked for and the error is unavoidable of considering the rise a sign of general reaction, whereas it has nothing to do with the mallein.

Of course, the syringe used should be surgically clean, and the mallein should be clear and without sediment. How long mallein will keep good and active is not, perhaps, known; kept under proper conditions, certainly six months and probably a year. But it is best to obtain fresh supplies, and these can always be in amount just sufficient to cover probable demands. Directions to wash and disinfect the skin of the neck before injecting are usually given, and obeyed in practice. I consider this a waste of time, and my experience is that if the skin be dry the results are invariably good.

When the temperature of a horse is normal and a sub-cutaneous injection of mallein is made we have a double reaction as an indication that he is infected with glanders. We have a rise of temperature from 100·5 to 104 or more, and we have a local swelling at the site of injection of four or more inches diameter.

The rise of temperature commences about seven hours after the injection is made and continues to increase up to about the sixteenth hour. If the horse be infected, the temperature may remain high for some hours longer, and in a few cases for some days.

The following is a typical reaction :—

	Temperature.	Diameter of Local Swelling.
Temperature at 8 p.m., time of injection	100	
„ 8 a.m., 12 hours after	104	3 inches
„ 12 m., 16 hours after	105	4 „
„ 4 p.m., 20 hours after	105	5 „
„ 8 p.m., 24 hours after	104	6 „

The local swelling develops gradually, and, when specific, increases in size for over the twenty-four hours following injection. Very little value attaches to the vertical measurement of a swelling, which results from the effusion gravitating. The typical swelling is round, raised well above the surrounding skin, painful on pressure, but above all one which increases in diameter after the twenty-fourth hour.

Although I accept a mallein reaction as specific of glanders, I must acknowledge that an ideal double reaction is not always given. Sometimes the rise of temperature is less than we consider indicative, whilst the swelling is typical. At others, the swelling is too little to offer any guidance, whilst the temperature is typically high.

A temperature rising from normal to 105° with a swelling of six inches in diameter, is an indication of glanders upon which slaughter may be safely advised. In an infected stud I should also accept a temperature of 104° with a four inch swelling, which increased or remained after the twenty-fourth hour, as signs of infection; so should I a temperature of 103° with a seven inch swelling, or a temperature of 105° with a three inch swelling.

There are imperfect reactions which render it difficult to draw a hard and fast line as to when a reaction may be positively accepted as indicative of glanders, and these have a very practical bearing now that the law recognises reaction to mallein as equivalent to " diseased."

As the exact time after injection at which the double reaction reaches its maximum is not definite, it becomes important to know when the horse should be examined—his temperature taken, and the swelling measured. I do not think any useful information is missed by not visiting the horse after injection until sixteen hours have elapsed. In a few cases the temperature may rise to 105 by the sixteenth hour and fall to 104 by the twenty-fourth, but that register is quite sufficient if the swelling is indicative; and as the swelling in an affected animal goes on increasing after the twenty-fourth hour, it is advisable not to make the concluding visit too early. There are very few definite reactions which need for their recognition more than one visit after injection, and that should be made on the twenty-fourth hour. To read the double reaction of mallein most accurately—to recognise the maximum temperature and see the full quantity and quality of the swelling—we must take the temperature at the time of injection, again at the sixteenth hour, and again when we examine the swelling at, or just after the twenty-fourth hour. The really indefinite reactions—temperature under 103 and swelling less than four inches—must be tested again, and this may best be done after a period of two or three weeks. I fix this time as the best, but I have seen perfect reactions when the injection has been repeated in a week. In cases which have reacted to mallein, a second test often shows a typical swelling, but a reduced rise in temperature. Here the swelling may be accepted as indicating disease, even if the temperature is only 103 or even a degree less. There are a few exceptional cases in which a rise of temperature occurs within twenty-four hours with no swelling, but in the next twenty-four hours a typical swelling develops. These cases are infected, and the possibility of this delayed local reaction should make us careful not to pronounce a horse free from glanders, if a rise of temperature has occurred before the lapse of forty-eight hours.

In cases of Purpura, I have said an injection of mallein may be followed by a large swelling, but it soon subsides. There are some artificially induced conditions which cause horses to give a local reaction to mallein. In the preparation of sera and antitoxins, horses are injected with various bacteria or bacterial products until they become immune. These immune horses will often give a large local reaction to mallein, but there is little or no rise in temperature. If there is a rise, it reaches its maximum more rapidly than in glanders and also declines more abruptly. The subject has been carefully considered by Messrs. H. I Sudmersen and A. J. Glenny, who published their experiments and conclusions in *The Journal of Hygiene*, Vol. 8, No. 1.

It is inadvisable to make a mallein test of a horse with a temperature over 102'5. In cases where diagnosis is urgent, and we test an animal with a temperature of 103 or higher, *a fall* of two degrees in 24 hours is a suspicious sign which may be considered in conjunction with the local swelling.

I have seen some reactions to mallein which were apparently misleading. I have heard of others from good observers. These results force one to acknowledge that the use of mallein is only an aid to diagnosis. There are cases in which mallein has given a typical reaction but a post mortem examination has failed to reveal any specific lesions. There are also cases in which mallein has failed to give a reaction whilst a post-mortem examination has disclosed definite glanders lesions. These misleading results are few and far between.

When a stud of horses that has been infected for some time is tested with mallein we expect to have a number of animals give a reaction, and a few to show an indefinite reaction. These latter are re-tested in ten to fourteen days, and those that react are killed. After this it is expected that the stud is clear, but it is not uncommon to find another case or two develop.

The probable explanation of this is that infection must reach a certain stage before it is indicated by mallein. Nocard infected a horse by ingestion of glanders bacilli, and injected mallein on the 7th, 14th and 21st days after. No reaction was given until the third test was made. If this experiment may be accepted as generally applicable, horses infected seven days before being injected with mallein would give no indication of their infection. In some horses experimentally infected by Sir J. M'Fadyean, a reaction to mallein was given thirteen days afterwards. We should probably be certain to detect all infected by repeating the test in any stud after the lapse of fourteen days. In a stud from which a number of clinical cases has recently been removed, the possibility of these undiscovered infections warns us that a re-test of the whole should be adopted if we desire to be quite certain that no disease remains.

A safe rule to adopt is—When in doubt repeat the test. No one asserts that mallein is infallible. It is to be accepted as an aid to diagnosis, and its reactions considered with the history and surroundings of the horse. But it is an aid far more reliable than any other, more trustworthy than any expert opinion, and indicative when no trace or sign of disease can be detected by the most careful clinical examination.

Experiments have been made with a view to determine whether repeated doses of mallein would confer any immunity against infection. Healthy horses have been injected with large doses, and with small doses repeated at intervals for weeks, but in no case was protection given against an inoculation with a pure culture of the bacilli.

Experiments have also been made to arrive at a positive answer to the question, "When a horse ceases to react to mallein, is he free from glanderous infection?" This question requires that we clearly understand what is meant by "Ceasing to react." It presumes that a horse has reacted to mallein once or more, and that he has not reacted to the last injection. If the injections were all made at short intervals, I should not accept the failure to react after the last injection as positive evidence of recovery and that no active bacilli remained in his tissues. But if the result of a number of injections had been a gradual abatement of the reaction until no reaction followed the mallein test, I should be strongly inclined to believe that the disease had ceased. If, further, after the lapse of two months from the last injection which gave no reaction, another test were made with no reaction, I should feel quite convinced that the horse had ceased to be infected, and was non-infective to others. This I accept as a "ceased reactor," and believe that no active bacilli reside in his tissues.

There is just one more point in relation to the use or abuse of mallein which requires notice. Can it be fraudulently used to disguise the existence of disease as revealed by a mallein test? In cases where the disease is not extensive, and has not developed any clinical signs, an injection of mallein gives a full reaction. In a number of such cases, if well fed and not overworked, a series of mallein tests, say once a month for three or four months, yield a gradually decreasing reaction. Whether this is due to the glanders lesions becoming sealed up and their contained bacilli dying, or to the general system failing to respond to an agent which it has got used to, I cannot say; but I am inclined to accept the first hypothesis, for many reasons. There are cases in which mallein repeated weekly has been followed by typical reactions every time the test was imposed. These animals on post-mortem show widely-disseminated nodules in the lungs, containing active bacilli. There are cases in which reaction to mallein ceases and the lungs show the ordinary nodular lesions, but a biological test reveals no active bacilli. In all cases where a post-mortem follows immediately upon a reaction to mallein, the lungs show hyperæmic patches and lines upon the pleura in the neighbourhood of nodules. This local reaction, I believe, assists the natural effort always going on in a healthy horse to surround and close a glanders nodule so that no bacilli escape. When horses are detected by one mallein test and isolated, they may live and work for months, some for years, without exhibiting clinical symptoms —but few of them, even a year or two after, will fail to react to an injection of mallein. Repeated monthly doses of mallein seem to have a further effect—that of assisting to seal the nodules and to imprison the bacilli, which ultimately die; and then no reaction to mallein occurs, even when the animals live for years.

I believe that no fraudulent use of mallein will disguise the condition of a horse if a week elapses between the test and the time of his previous injection. If a horse is infected there will be sufficient reaction to give rise to suspicion, but care must be taken to detect the maximum rise in temperature, and that necessitates at least two observations—one at the 16th hour and another at the 24th. The reaction given by a glandered horse to a mallein test is less well marked after repeated doses of mallein than if none had been used.

The following are the directions sent out with mallein issued from the Royal Veterinary College.

DIRECTIONS FOR USING MALLEIN.

1. While under the mallein test, horses ought to be left at rest in the stable and protected from draughts. The rectal temperature ought to be taken once or twice on the day before the test is applied.

2. The dose of mallein for a horse is one cubic centimetre, or 18 minims. It ought to be injected about the middle of the side of the neck, with a clean hypodermic syringe. The best form of syringe is one with an asbestos piston, as the whole instrument may then be sterilised by boiling it in water for five minutes before use.

3. The mallein must be injected into the subcutaneous connective tissue, and care must be taken that the whole dose is actually introduced.

4. The temperature must be taken at the time of injection, and at the 9th, 12th, and 15th hours afterwards.

5. Provided the temperature was normal (under 101° F.) before the injection, it will rise 2° or more (103°—105°) during the next 15 hours if the horse is glandered, but it will remain practically unaffected (under 102°) if the horse is not glandered.

6. Attention must also be paid to the swelling that forms at the seat of injection. When the horse is glandered this goes on increasing in size during the second 24 hours after the injection, and it seldom declines before the 3rd or 4th day. The maximum diameter of this swelling in glandered horses varies from 5 to 10 inches.

7. In horses that are not glandered the local swelling attains its maximum size during the first 15 hours, and by the 24th hour it has almost entirely disappeared. Its maximum diameter is usually about 3 or 4 inches.

8. When the temperature gradually rises from the normal to 104° during the first 15 hours, and a large slowly-disappearing swelling forms at the seat of injection, the horse may confidently be declared glandered.

9. If, with a normal temperature at the time of injection, a horse displays only the temperature reaction, or only the local reaction, the case must be considered doubtful, and the test repeated after the lapse of a week.

10. When the temperature is 102° or more at the time of injection, the temperature reaction is unreliable, but in such a case the diagnosis may be based on the characters of the local swelling.

11. The mallein should be kept in a cool place, and protected from light. Should it lose its transparency, or become cloudy, it must not be used.

CURE AND RECOVERY

A considerable experience of glanders warrants me in saying that very few cases of clinically developed disease recover or are cured. When the treatment of glanders was attempted—and it generally was before the 1878 Order, there were many partial or temporary cures, but nearly all in a short time developed further symptoms and had to be slaughtered. The cases most amenable to treatment were certainly those of the cutaneous form, and among the most rapid recoveries were cases which showed only a chain of farcy buds joined by a cord. The treatment adopted was to force into each bud a red hot iron, and success—at any rate for a time—seemed to have been attained. It is just possible that many of these were cases in which the lesions marked the point of infection, and that the bacilli never reached the lungs.

Many of our older practitioners can tell of cases which lived and worked for years after such recoveries without developing any further sign of the disease. Even in cases where ulcers were visible on the nasal mucosa apparent recovery sometimes occurred, and cicatrices marked the spot upon which an ulcer had healed.

I must confess that even those temporary recoveries were but a small proportion of those treated. One bay mare that showed an enlarged sub-maxillary gland and a hind leg much swollen, with two or three "buds" on it, became free from all clinical signs in about three months. It then worked eight years in an omnibus without any sign of disease, and was off work from lameness when mallein was first introduced into this country. It was tested, and reacted violently. On recovering from the lameness it resumed work for a year, when further defects in its limbs rendered it useless, and I had an opportunity given me of making a post-mortem examination. Before slaughtering the mare, we tried another mallein test and a typical reaction resulted. The post-mortem revealed glanderous lungs with many old calcareous nodules and a large extent of fibroid change. Had the mallein test not been available during life, no one could have had any suspicion that the mare was not a sound animal.

The favourite drugs used in the treatment of glanders were iron, copper and arsenic. They certainly had some beneficial effect, if only for an uncertain period. Rest and good feeding were essential—even to temporary recovery. The horse that worked hard whilst suffering from latent glanders, as a rule, was not many months before again exhibiting clinical symptoms.

Since mallein has come into use it has disclosed the existence of latent glanders to an extent that was never suspected, and it is a question whether many of these cases in which infection is limited to one or two small pulmonary centres may not spontaneously recover, as do some cases of tuberculosis. There are certainly some well authenticated cases in which horses have given a typical reaction to mallein, have continued at work for years, and have shown no clinical development of the disease. As only one dose of mallein was used, it can hardly be said that the recovery was due to any curative effect of that agent. It may be that a spontaneous recovery had taken place and, as few post-mortem examinations of such cases are recorded, it may be that the disease still existed in a latent form. There are other cases in which mallein has been used, not only to diagnose the presence of disease, but to arrive at a decision as to its remaining active. Many of these continued to react to every test and may be safely accepted as suffering from latent glanders due to living bacilli in the body. When, however, horses cease to react to repeated doses of mallein, work for years, and then fail to give any reaction to mallein, we assume that they have recovered.

In some experiments conducted for the Board of Agriculture in the year 1903, six horses, which two years before had reacted to mallein, and since then worked every day, were re-tested and failed to give any reaction. These horses were turned loose with six healthy horses into a large barn, and the whole twelve kept there for a year, using a common water trough and one long manger. At the end of the time all were killed. The healthy horses showed no sign of infection during life and no glanders lesions after death. The ceased reactors all showed some old nodules which were biologically tested by Sir John M'Fadyean, who failed to find any active bacilli in the lungs of any of the six animals. I think only one conclusion can be drawn from this experiment, viz.: that under certain favourable circumstances, in which mallein played a part, recovery from glanders took place. The resisting power of the horse is only one factor concerned in the recovery from glanders—the quantity and quality of the infecting bacilli is another. Probably many horses would recover if they were well fed and not worked. But the horse is kept for work, and this renders recovery almost impossible.

Of course, treatment is out of the question since the issue of the 1907 Order. Cases must be reported and killed. If 30 per cent. of recoveries in such latent cases as can only be discovered by mallein could be anticipated, it would not be worth while making the attempt. To say nothing of the loss of work, the failure of the 70 per cent., and the continued infection which would result, we should never clear the kingdom of the plague, as there is every reason to expect we shall do by enforcing the existing law.

Cures of, or recoveries from, glanders are so few and far between that they may be treated as of scientific interest, but not as useful facts of any benefit to horse owners. Their pursuit in the past was fraught with disappointment, and was a powerful factor in obstructing the acceptance of the only effective preventive action—slaughtering every case as soon as detected.

PREVENTION.

The prevention of glanders requires intelligent action upon the part of horse-owners on their premises and with their studs; it also requires well considered regulations to be enforced by all local authorities, and supervision over the whole by a central body, such as the Board of Agriculture.

A private individual may, at considerable expense and after continuous efforts, clear his stud of glanders, but so long as his neighbour has infected stables and horses, he is liable to the re-introduction of disease and its spread through his own stud.

A local authority cannot enforce regulations unless these are granted by State legislation, and has no power beyond its own geographical boundary. The best efforts of an authority are neutralised by want of action in the surrounding districts, and so it is necessary that regulations for the whole country shall be general and uniform.

A central State authority is essential for the guidance and control of all the local authorities. A central authority is capable of effectively dealing with a contagious disease among animals directly, without the interposition of a local authority, but this entails the establishment of an army of inspectors who cannot act with the promptness of men on the spot. A still greater objection to centralised action is that it destroys the interest of the local stock-owners and authorities, who become careless, and having no authority are unwilling to assume any responsibility. Some diseases, such as cattle-plague and swine fever, that appear suddenly, spread rapidly, and are carried by other means than the visibly diseased animal, are best suppressed by central action. Others, such as glanders and tuberculosis, having long periods of latency and less rapidity of spread, are most surely controlled by local action.

In Great Britain the Diseases of Animals Acts are administered by a central authority—the Board of Agriculture—assisted by local authorities. The owners of stock and their private veterinary advisers also play an important part in co-operating, or otherwise, with the authorities.

The discovery of disease is a matter antecedent to all preventive action; and the owners or their veterinary surgeons must be trusted to make this discovery first, and then to notify its existence. The prevention of all the scheduled diseases, as well as those not yet scheduled, must commence in the stable, field or shed.

When a stable is free from glanders, and has been so for years, the owner can hardly be expected to take extra precautions against the introduction of disease. His long freedom is evidence that he does not purchase in a district where glanders prevails, and that his horses do not associate with those likely to be infective. Buying young horses in country districts is almost free from the danger of introducing glanders into a stud. There is no permanent infection of country districts. But clean-looking young horses suffering from latent glanders have been detected in towns a few days after their arrival. The explanation is nearly always the same; the horse had been previously sold to a town customer on approval, had been delivered, and after a week or two returned as not suitable. Unknown, perhaps, to anyone, he had been infected and then sent back to the country suffering from latent glanders. Not many such cases occur, but I have known more than one, and they reveal a danger against which it is difficult to guard.

Horses kept by private individuals for harness or saddle work very seldom suffer from glanders—not because they are immune, but simply because they do not come in contact with glandered horses. But private stables are not exempt from glanders. I have notes of two or three cases in which glanders has appeared in a private stable and in which the source of infection was only discovered by accident. In nearly all these the infection resulted from standing the horse at livery whilst the owner was on a visit to friends, and the origin was only discovered by finding that at the time of the visit glanders existed in the livery stable.

It is apparent then that so long as glanders prevails around us, the most careful owner of horses may be unable to protect himself against infection. He may introduce the disease by a new purchase suffering from the latent stage of glanders, or he may have one of his old horses infected through the mangers or pails used in another stable by a diseased horse.

The owner who has a large stud and has to make frequent purchases to maintain it in working order may guard himself against the introduction of disease by the new horse suffering from latent infection, by testing with mallein every new purchase soon after its arrival. No one can absolutely provide against contagion if his horses cohabit with others that are infected, and therefore it is the interest of all horse owners to assist in stamping out the disease throughout the kingdom.

The man who buys cast horses from large studs, or who buys at sales, should always test every new purchase within twenty-four hours of receiving it into his stable. If it reacts, he can demand the return of his money when a warranty of soundness has been given—but in no other case. At the worst, he protects the rest of his horses from infection, and probably may be able to come to some compromise with the vendor. If it became a general practice for horse-buyers to test their new purchases, the custom would have a most beneficial effect in preventing the spread of disease, because owners would then hesitate to sell any horse which would, if diseased, be detected at once by the purchaser.

When a stud is already infected—and many in London have been so for fifty years—the most essential preventive action is to find out which horses are diseased. This can be done by applying the mallein test to the whole. To make doubly sure that no infected horse has escaped detection, the test should be repeated in six or eight weeks. All that react must be separated from the healthy, and isolated, if not slaughtered immediately.

With a large stud stabled in widely distant depôts, the full value of testing with mallein may be lost through carelessness in changing horses from depôt to depôt. A horse moved from one stable to another without having been first tested may carry disease, and spread it widely before being detected. An oversight of this kind has been the means of reinfecting more than one stable.

Turning horses out to grass, at any rate on farms round London, has been a fruitful source of infection. Horses from different stables run together, and there may be as many as twenty or thirty horses in one set of meadows. I knew a case in which eighteen horses were attacked with glanders within four months of being at grass. The infection was traced to one old horse not worth £10. The owners of pastures round London should admit no horses to their fields unless from a known clean stable, or after a test with mallein has been made. London horse-owners would be well advised not to turn out their horses, except with a guarantee from the farmer that no strange horses are allowed to run with them.

It is evident that whenever horses are collected together in numbers from various places, there is a chance that an animal suffering from latent glanders may be among them. The accommodation at large fairs and race meetings favours infection spreading if a diseased horse should happen to be present. Military manœuvres have often helped to spread glanders, not by infection from the well-looked-after army horses, but by a diseased animal introduced with the mixed lot supplied by contractors.

War, of course, always spreads glanders among the troop and transport horses, but the spread does not cease with the war, and is not confined to the army. As soon as peace is declared, economy suggests the sale of superfluous horses, and thousands of infected animals are in this way scattered over the whole country in which the war took place. Since mallein became available for testing horses, the dissemination of glanders by sale of cast horses is no longer excusable, and I am glad to say that in South Africa very great care was taken to guard against the sale of infected animals—thousands of doses of mallein having been used to protect stockowners who bought the superfluous horses.

One of the most important preventive measures to be taken by authorities engaged in stamping out glanders is to trace back the history of infected horses, and attempt to discover the source of their infection. The relation of a concrete case or two will make this point clear.

A glandered horse is found in a cab-yard, and the owner states he has never before had any disease. The history of the horse is that he was purchased at a sale ten days before he was noticed to be ill. At the sale-yard the name and address of the vendor are obtained, and his stud is inspected—it consists of 17 horses; one showing slightly suspicious symptoms is tested with mallein, reacts and is killed. The post-mortem reveals old glanders lesions. Then the remainder of the stud is tested, and five horses react, which are found glandered on post-mortem. From the first case we were able to find six dangerous animals, and put a stop to further infection.

A dead horse is found in a knacker's yard with glanders nodules in the lungs. On going to the stable from which he came there are seen eight horses, none of which show any clinical symptoms of glanders, but all are rather poor in condition and aged. The lot were tested, and every one reacted—their infective condition being proved by post-mortem examination.

A greengrocer notified that a pony of his was suspicious. It was found glandered. He bought it the week before from a small dealer. The dealer's stable was visited and found to contain four horses. The mallein test showed no reaction in any of them. The greengrocer's pony had only been on these premises one night, and had been bought from a stranger at the Cattle Market. Further history could not be obtained.

A horse in a well-managed stud was found with farcy. The animal had been there two years, and no case of glanders had been seen in the stud. The history of the horse included two months' at grass for lameness, and he had only resumed work about a month. The field was in another authority's district, so application was made to the veterinary inspector of the district, and he replied that he had seen four cases of glanders on the farm at which the horse had been grazing.

When the spread of infection can be traced to its source an unnotified outbreak is often discovered—it may, or may not, be one known to the owner.

One of the cases I have referred to was discovered in a knacker's yard; and if these places were inspected by the veterinary surgeons of all local authorities, as they are in London, many cases of glanders would be found that now escape detection.

Around the metropolis are a number of horse-slaughterers' establishments which are never inspected, and to which London owners may send dead or diseased horses without notification if they desire to hide the condition of their stables. It is unfair to the London Authorities that neighbouring County Councils should neglect so obvious a danger to themselves, and so handy a method of hiding disease for the dishonest horse-owner who wishes to evade notification.

The law once required notification from all horse-slaughterers of cases of glanders coming to their establishments. They only notified those cases which were condemned by an inspector of a local authority,

and when asked why they notified no others, replied, " We are not
veterinary surgeons, and do not recognise half-developed cases." Even
occasional surprise visits to knackers' yards by the veterinary inspectors
of Local Authorities would do good, by checking the practice of sending
glandered horses for destruction without notifying them to the police, and
also by the detection of some of the unknown outbreaks from which
these diseased animals are surreptitiously removed.

It has been suggested that public sales and auctions should be inspected by the official veterinary inspector. If clinically-diseased horses
were ever sold there, inspection would be valuable--but they are not.
The horses entering every horse-repository in London are examined by
the auctioneers' private veterinary surgeon—and very strictly examined.
The horses coming through repositories that help to spread glanders are
those in which the disease is latent, and may remain latent for a long
time.   To inspect these and pass them would inspire many buyers with a
sense of security that was more apparent than real ; and when the latent
disease developed shortly after purchase, the same class of buyer would
feel great contempt for the inspector who had not discovered that the
horse was infected.

The sanitary condition of some stables is a disgrace to civilisation.
Horses are over-crowded, badly fed, over-worked, and in many places
unable to lie down for rest.   But glanders prevails no more in this class
of stable than in those where sanitary rules are observed.   In the bad
stables a case of glanders at its commencement is more apt to be overlooked than in well-managed stables.   It may therefore infect other
horses before it is diagnosed.   In the insanitary stable it is usual to find
other branches of management defective, and particularly so as to the
hours of work, weight of load, and pace on a journey.   These evils
combined cause glanders to develop much more rapidly than under more
favourable conditions, with the result that poor owners who carry on
business under such conditions only want one outbreak of glanders in
their stables to invite bankruptcy.   I could point to scores of such cases
in London.

Disinfection and cleanliness are enforced by law in all stables which
have been the scene of a glanders outbreak.   This application must not
be confined to the mangers, walls, and floors.   Nose-bags, pails and

stable utensils must all be disinfected, if not destroyed. Rugs and halters, if they are worth saving, may be soaked in a solution of carbolic acid and hung to dry in the sun for a day or two. Before any disinfection is done the place should be made as clean as possible. Mangers must be emptied and with the stalls, walls, and bales soaked with a few pailfuls of water over night; then hot water and soda applied with a brush until the grain of the wood is visible. After a day or two to dry, the walls, etc. may be dressed with hot lime wash. The floors and manure are best treated with dry quick lime.

Of course, no prevention of glanders is real which does not aim at stamping the disease out of the country. This means the slaughter of every case as soon as it is diagnosed. Before mallein was discovered, it would have been a long and expensive task to have cleared the country of glanders. By the use of mallein we may now clear all infected studs; but it must be remembered that the most careful use of this agent will not always indicate every infected horse in a stud throughout which glanders has been long and widely distributed. Until a horse has been infected for ten or twelve days, an injection of mallein may give no reaction, and therefore diseased animals may escape detection when the stud is only submitted to one test. These undetected cases will in time develop, and form fresh centres for the distribution of disease.

Professor Bang long since pointed out, in the case of tuberculosis, how herds which had been tested with tuberculin and from which all reactors had been removed, when re-tested a few months later disclosed a small percentage of infection which had escaped the first test. A similar experience is found with glanders, and is likely to be even more noticeable in stables from which animals that give an indefinite reaction are not removed. It is well to remember this, because the expectation of an easy and prompt clearance of disease from a large stud may lead to disappointment, and both owners and officials become disheartened and sceptical.

The stamping-out of any disease is a laborious process, and mistakes are certain to occur—every mistake may give rise to a fresh outbreak.

The Order of 1907, will, I believe, prove successful, but local authorities would do well to arrange with owners of large studs, which are supposed to have been freed from disease by mallein testing and slaughter, for a second test of all the horses a month or two after the slaughter of the last reactor.

Importation. Considering the trouble and expense devoted to clearing our home stock, it is right that provision should be made against the introduction of glanders from other countries. The new Order imposes a very mild regulation upon horses, asses and mules —they shall not be landed unless accompanied by a veterinary certificate to the effect that they show no symptom of disease. Experience proves that not much risk is run by importing a good class of young horse ; but a few infected horses have arrived, and others may arrive. When we have cleared our own studs, the Board of Agriculture will probably enforce the use of the mallein test upon imported horses.

LEGISLATION.

State legislation for the control or suppression of glanders is necessary because the efforts of individuals can only apply to their own studs. After prolonged and expensive action, a horse-owner may be successful in stamping out the disease in his stables, but when glanders is allowed to prevail around him he is never safe, and sooner or later is almost certain to again find his stud infected.

State legislation should be uniform and general ; it should be compulsory—not permissive. When the latter, we have authorities in one part doing little, and in another part performing an expensive task which is rendered unsuccessful by re-invasion of disease from the district which neglects its duty.

Legislation should not be all penal. With penalties for offences it should combine rewards for assistance. It is a misfortune, not a crime, for a man to have his animals affected with glanders. To get rid of the disease legislation must interfere with his use of horses which may be of great intrinsic value to him, and of no injury to his neighbour. It must destroy horses which present no sign of disease, and which, though infected, may never become infective. To meet these cases, compulsory slaughter of stock should be accompanied by monetary compensation. The argument for compensation in cases where legislation is directed, with probable success, to eradicating a disease from the country is not on the same level as a claim for trade losses due to unpreventable accidents. These accidents will occur again no matter what care and cost is expended on them. But success in stamping out disease means the permanent freedom from the loss caused by such disease, and therefore a national loss is saved which far exceeds the national contribution in the form of compensation. Legislation must not be in advance of intelligent public opinion. If it is, there is resistance, active or passive, which renders the regulations a failure. When owners of stock acknowledge the value of legislation nearly everyone interested co-operates, and success is assured. There are, of course, always some owners who will attempt evasion, and a few who wilfully spread disease by moving or selling diseased animals. For such the penal clauses are requisite. Legislation fails in its object when weak half-measures are adopted—their want of success, with the accompaniment of hardship to owners from rigid restrictions, brings the whole of the legislative measures into disrepute.

Legislation in regard to glanders has been a very slow and weak thing in Great Britain. It began with mild measures against the worst forms of spreading disease, and very gradually, during 50 years, advanced to the conditions which now promise success.

In 1853 an Act of Parliament prohibited bringing glandered horses into markets, and turning them out on unenclosed lands.

In 1869 the Contagious Disease (Animals) Act scheduled glanders as a contagious disease, and provided for the compulsory burial of carcases of horses affected with glanders. Under this Act the Privy Council were given power to issue Orders which should have all the effect of the Act.

In 1873 by an Order of Council farcy was included amongst the diseases scheduled under the Act, but simply for the prevention of movement of diseased horses.

In 1878 an amended Contagious Diseases (Animals) Act was passed, and by an Order under it glanders and farcy were made "diseases," and horses, mules and asses "animals," under the provisions of the Act. Thus compulsory notification of glanders and farcy was introduced, local authorities were empowered to make regulations as to movement, and owners were required to slaughter horses suffering from glanders, and to isolate those suffering from farcy.

In 1892 an Order was issued by the Board of Agriculture making glanders and farcy one disease for legislative purposes, and giving local authorities power to slaughter on payment of compensation. The compensation was fixed at half the value of the horse, with a limit of £20.

The result of this Order was that the largest local authorities declined to slaughter, holding that the cost imposed was too great.

In 1894 another Order superseded that of 1892. Slaughter was still permissive, and accompanied by compensation on a lower scale, viz., one-fourth the value of the horse or such smaller sum as the authorities saw fit to pay, but not less than £2 per horse.

This Order made compulsory :—

> Notification of the disease by the owner or person in charge.
> Inspection by Local Authorities' officers.
> Prohibition of movement or exposure of diseased animals.
> Disinfection of place in which disease has existed.

It permitted local authorities to make regulations for :—

> Slaughter and payment of compensation.
> Disposal of carcases, manure, forage, litter, etc.
> Movement of diseased or suspected animals.
> Movement of animals into or out of any stable or other place in which glanders exists, or which have been in contact with any diseased or suspected horse.

Of course permissive powers are of no avail unless a local authority use them, and some did not. The regulation as to the movement of horses in contact with diseased horses would have been most valuable if it had not been rendered nugatory by a proviso as follows :—" It shall operate so long only as a diseased animal remains on the premises, and until the regulations as to cleansing and disinfection have been carried out." In other words, as soon as a glandered horse had been slaughtered and removed, the inspector had no more power in that stable, though he might feel certain that a fourth of the horses therein were infected animals.

This Order was soon found to be ineffective, as it did not control the movement of latent cases of glanders, and the disease continued to prevail widely. Fortunately mallein, an aid to diagnosis, had been discovered, and many veterinary practitioners commenced to use it by testing their in-contact horses, and so guarding against the danger of latent disease being unexpectedly developed.

Under the Order of 1894 little progress was made, and the returns to the Board of Agriculture showed no settled reduction either in the number of outbreaks or in the number of animals attacked. It became evident that no real success in controlling the disease, still less in suppressing it, could be expected so long as slaughter was merely permissive, and the in-contact horses were altogether ignored as potentially dangerous animals. Mallein had been well tried by veterinarians, and its value appreciated, but the laws gave it no recognition, and its use, denied to the official veterinary inspector, was left to the discretion of owners and their private veterinary advisers.

In 1899 a Departmental Committee was appointed by the Board of Agriculture, with Lord Stanley as Chairman. It took evidence, and issued recommendations; still legislation remained the same, and it was not till 1907 that a new Order, based on the 1899 Committee's suggestions, and in accordance with modern veterinary science came into force. The recommendations of the Committee were as follows:—

1. That the Board of Agriculture should exercise a more extended supervision of the working of the Glanders or Farcy Order.

2. That the Glanders or Farcy Order should be amended to permit of notification of disease being made either to a constable or a veterinary inspector.

3. That where practicable the local veterinary inspector should not engage in private practice.

4. That it should be made obligatory for veterinary surgeons to notify cases of glanders of which they become aware.

5. That occupiers or owners of knackers' yards should notify any case of glanders found in animals taken to their yards for slaughter.

6. That horses that react to the mallein test should be considered as possible sources of infection.

7. That horses that the Veterinary Inspector may consider to have been exposed to contagion should be dealt with in the same manner as suspected horses, but with certain reservations.

8. That the slaughter of all animals showing "clinical" symptoms of glanders should be made compulsory.

9. That compensation for horses slaughtered solely on account of reaction to the mallein test should be on a higher scale than that for a

"clinically" diseased horse, with a limit of £25. But in the event of no glanders lesions being found post-mortem the compensation should be the full value, with a limit of £50.

10. That the Board of Agriculture should conduct experiments with regard to the use and influence of mallein.

During the years immediately following 1899 no fresh legislation was attempted, but it gradually dawned upon our rulers that something would have to be done. The spread of glanders among horses continued and increased. Deaths among men began to attract some notice, and it was shown that whereas the Registrar-General returned about 6 or 7 fatal cases from human glanders per annum, a larger number were probably never recognised, but registered for burial as typhoid or influenza, or rheumatic fever, or blood-poisoning.

There is very little doubt that ten times as many human deaths from glanders have occurred as have been accredited to that cause by the Registrar-General.

Deputations from local authorities waited upon Presidents of the Board of Agriculture, and met with civility but no assistance. Glasgow and London simply begged for more power to control glanders, but they had to wait.

By 1905 the Board of Agriculture had really grasped the facts of the case, and tentatively drew a new Order. Then the Board endeavoured to obtain some financial assistance from the National Treasury, knowing that any earnest attempt to stamp out glanders would be attended by expense—greater expense than could honestly be inflicted upon local rates. The Treasury declined to assist, and in 1907 the Board issued the new Order, leaving local authorities to do the work and pay for it.

THE GLANDERS OR FARCY ORDER OF 1907.

The Board of Agriculture and Fisheries, by virtue and in exercise of the powers vested in them under the Diseases of Animals Acts, 1894 to 1903, and of every other power enabling them in this behalf, do order, and it is hereby ordered, as follows:

Definition of "Disease" "Diseased" and "Suspected."

1.—(1). For the purposes of this Order disease means glanders, and includes that form of glanders which is commonly known as farcy.

(2). A diseased horse, ass, or mule means for the purposes of this Order a horse, ass, or mule in which the clinical symptoms are definite evidence of disease, or in which the application of the mallein test has resulted in definite evidence of disease.

(3). An animal shall be deemed to be "suspected," if it shows clinical symptoms of disease but such symptoms are insufficient to make the animal a diseased animal within the definition of this Article.

Regulation of Importation of Horses, Asses, and Mules.

2. No horse, ass, or mule, brought to Great Britain from any other country, except Ireland, the Channel Islands, or the Isle of Man, shall be landed in Great Britain unless it is accompanied by a certificate of a veterinary surgeon to the effect that he examined the animal immediately before it was embarked or whilst it was on board the vessel, as the case may be, and that he found that the animal did not show symptoms of disease.

Notice of Disease.

3.—(1). Every person having or having had in his possession, or under his charge any diseased or suspected horse, ass, or mule shall with all practicable speed give notice of the fact of the horse, ass, or mule being or having been so diseased or suspected to a constable of the police force for the police area wherein the diseased or suspected horse, ass, or mule is or was.

(2). Every person licensed to slaughter horses who has in his possession a carcase of any diseased or suspected horse, ass, or mule shall with all practicable speed give notice of that fact to a constable of the police force for the police area wherein the carcase is.

(3). The constable receiving the notice shall forthwith give information of the receipt by him of the notice to an Inspector of the Local Authority, who shall forthwith report the same to the Local Authority, and also to the Medical Officer of Health of the Sanitary District in which the animal died or was slaughtered or in which the carcase was at the time of the notice.

(4). Where the notice of disease relates to a carcase of an animal that has died or been slaughtered in the district of a Local Authority other than the Local Authority which receives the notice, the latter shall forthwith inform the other Local Authority of the receipt of the notice.

Duty of Inspector to act immediately.

4. An Inspector of a Local Authority on receiving in any manner whatsoever information of the supposed existence of disease, or having reasonable ground to suspect the existence of disease, shall proceed with all practicable speed to the place where the disease, according to the information received by him, exists, or is suspected to exist, and shall there and elsewhere put in force and discharge the powers and duties conferred and imposed on him as Inspector by or under the Act of 1894, and this Order.

Public Warning as to the Existence of Disease.

5.—(1). The Local Authority may if they think fit give public warning by placards, advertisement, or otherwise, of the existence of disease in any stable, building, field, or other place with or without any particular description thereof, as they think fit, and may continue to do so during the existence of the disease, and, in the case of a stable, building, or other like place, until the same has been cleansed and disinfected.

(2). It shall not be lawful for any person (without authority or excuse) to remove or deface any such placard.

Slaughter of Diseased Animals.

6. A Local Authority shall with all practicable speed cause to be slaughtered any horse, ass, or mule which is diseased.

Detention and Treatment of Animals in Contact with Disease or Suspected of Disease.

7.—(1). The provisions of this Article shall apply to any horse, ass, or mule which was suspected or which is or has been in contact, or in the same stable, building, field, or other place with a horse, ass, or mule which was then diseased.

(2). The Local Authority may cause a Notice (in the Form A set forth in the First Schedule to this Order or to the like effect) to be served on the owner or person in charge of any animal to which this Article applies, requiring the detention of the animal in the stable, building, field, or other place, where the animal is at the date of the service of the Notice, either unconditionally or subject to such conditions with a view to identification and the prevention of contact with other animals as may be prescribed in the Notice; and after the service of such Notice it shall be unlawful to move any animal to which it relates in contravention of the terms of such Notice.

(3). The Local Authority shall cause a Notice under this Article to be served in relation to every horse, ass, or mule which in their opinion has been exposed to the risk of contagion.

(4). The Local Authority may, with the written consent of the owner of the animal, apply the mallein test to any animal detained under this Article, and they shall apply the test to any such animal as soon as practicable after being so requested by the owner. The application of the test shall be made by a Veterinary Inspector of the Local Authority.

(5).—(i.) Where the application of the test by the Local Authority results in definite evidence of disease in an animal, it shall be slaughtered by the Local Authority with all practicable speed.

(ii.) Where in the opinion of the Veterinary Inspector the application results in indications of the disease not amounting to definite evidence of disease, the test shall be applied a second time not later than twelve days after the previous application.

(iii.) Where in the opinion of the Veterinary Inspector the original application results in no indications of the disease, or the second application does not result in definite evidence of disease, the Notice served under this Article shall cease to operate as regards the animal tested at the expiration of forty-eight hours after the application of the test.

(iv). The result of an application of the test shall forthwith be communicated in writing by the Veterinary Inspector to the owner or person in charge of the animal tested.

(6). Subject to the provisions of this Article a Notice hereunder may at any time be withdrawn by the Local Authority by service on the owner or person in charge of the animal of a Notice in the Form B set forth in the First Schedule to this Order or to the like effect.

(7). An Inspector shall with all practicable speed send copies of any Notice served by him under this Article to the Local Authority, and to the police officer in charge of the nearest police station of the District.

Appeal to Board of Agriculture and Fisheries against Order for Slaughter.

8. If the owner of any horse, ass, or mule gives notice in writing to the Local Authority, or to their Inspector or other officer, that he objects to the horse, ass, or mule being slaughtered under the provisions of this Order, it shall not be lawful for the Local Authority to cause that horse, ass, or mule to be slaughtered except with the special authority of the Board first obtained.

Post-mortem Examination of Slaughtered Animals.

9.—(1.) In the case of every animal slaughtered under this Order, in which at the time of slaughter the clinical symptoms are not definite evidence of disease, the carcase shall as soon as practicable be examined by a Veterinary Inspector of the Local Authority. Notice of intention to make such examination shall be given to the owner of the animal, who shall be entitled to be present at the examination in person or by a representative who, if the owner thinks fit, may be a veterinary surgeon.

(2). The Veterinary Inspector shall at the conclusion of his examination give to the owner of the animal or his representative at the examination a statement of the result of the examination in the Form C set forth in the First Schedule hereto or to the like effect.

(3). Where the owner of the animal or his representative is a veterinary surgeon, and in his opinion the decision of the Veterinary Inspector is incorrect, he may at or immediately after the examination require that the question as to the existence of disease shall be submitted to the Veterinary Officers of the Board, and in such case the Veterinary Inspector shall forthwith send to the Laboratory of the Board of Agriculture and Fisheries, Great Scotland Yard, London, S.W., all the materials necessary to enable those Officers to consider the question together with a copy of his statement of the result of the examination.

(4). A statement of the result of the examination signed by the Veterinary Inspector, or where there is a reference to the Veterinary Officers of the Board then a statement in the Form C set forth in the First Schedule hereto or to the like effect signed by one of such Veterinary Officers, shall for the purposes of this Order be conclusive evidence as to the result of the examination.

Compensation for Slaughter.

10.—(1). Where the veterinary examination under the preceding Article does not show that the animal was affected with glanders, the Local Authority shall out of the local rate pay as compensation for the animal the full value of the animal immediately before it received the mallein test, but the sum paid shall not exceed fifty pounds for any horse or twelve pounds for any ass or mule.

(2). When the veterinary examination shows that the animal was affected with glanders the Local Authority shall out of the local rate pay as compensation for the animal one-half of the value of the animal immediately before it received the mallein test, but the sum paid shall not exceed twenty-five pounds for any horse, or six pounds for any ass or mule.

(3). Where there is no veterinary examination under the preceding Article the Local Authority shall out of the local rate pay as compensation for an animal slaughtered under this Order such sum as the Local Authority think expedient, being a minimum of two pounds in the case of a horse and of ten shillings in the case of an ass or mule : Provided that in no case shall the amount of compensation, if above the said minimum, exceed one-fourth of the value of the animal immediately before it became diseased.

(4). The value of an animal for the purpose of compensation shall, in case of dispute, be determined in manner provided by the Animals (Transit and General) Amendment Order of 1904.

Regulations as to Marking Diseased and Suspected Animals.

11.—A Local Authority may make such Regulations as they think fit for prescribing and regulating the marking of diseased or suspected horses, asses, or mules.

Regulations of Local Authority as to Cleansing and Disinfection.

12.—(1). A Local Authority may make such Regulations as they think fit for the following purposes, or any of them :

(i.) for providing for the cleansing and disinfection of places used by, and of utensils, mangers, feeding-troughs, pens, hurdles, or other things used for or about, any diseased horse, ass, or mule :

(ii.) for providing for the cleansing and disinfection of vans or carts or other vehicles used for carrying any diseased horse, ass, or mule on land otherwise than on a railway :

(iii.) for prescribing the mode in which such cleansing and such disinfection are to be effected :

(iv.) for providing that such places, utensils, mangers, feeding-troughs, pens, hurdles, or other things, vans, carts, or other vehicles, are to be cleansed and disinfected at the expense of the Local Authority, or of the owner, lessee, or occupier thereof:

(v.) for regulating the taking out of any stable, building, field, or other place of any fodder, litter, or other thing that has been in contact with or used for or about any diseased horse, ass, or mule ; and

(vi.) for requiring the removal by the owner from contact with horses, asses, or mules, of litter used for or about any diseased horse, ass, or mule.

(2). The mode of disinfection shall be one of those prescribed by Article one of the Diseases of Animals (Disinfection) Order of 1906.

(3). If any person fails to cleanse and disinfect any place, or any utensil, manger, feeding-trough, pen, hurdle, or other thing, or any van, cart, or other vehicle in accordance with any such Regulation, it shall be lawful for the Local Authority, without prejudice to the recovery of any penalty for the infringement of such Regulation, to cause such place, or such utensil, manger, feeding-trough, pen, hurdle, or other thing, or such van, cart, or other vehicle to be cleansed and disinfected, or to remove such litter and to recover the expenses thereby incurred from such person in any court of competent jurisdiction.

Occupiers and Owners to give facilities for Cleansing, &c.

13.—Where the power of causing any place or any utensil, manger, feeding-trough, pen, hurdle, or other thing, or any van, cart, or other vehicle to be cleansed and disinfected under this Order is exercised by a Local Authority, the occupier or owner thereof shall give all reasonable facilities for that purpose.

Prohibition to expose or move Diseased Horses, Asses, or Mules.

14.—(1). It shall not be lawful for any person—

(i.) to expose a diseased horse, ass, or mule in a market, fair, sale-yard, or other public or private place where horses are commonly exposed for sale ;

(ii.) to place a diseased horse, ass, or mule in a lair or other place adjacent to or connected with a market, fair, or sale-yard, or where horses are commonly placed before exposure for sale ;

(iii.) to send or carry, or cause to be sent or carried, a diseased horse, ass, or mule on a railway, canal, river, or inland navigation, or in a coasting vessel ;

(iv.) to carry, lead, or drive, or cause to be carried, led, or driven, a diseased horse, ass, or mule on a highway or thoroughfare, except in accordance with the provisions of this Order ;

(v.) to place or keep a diseased horse, ass, or mule on common or unenclosed land, or in a field or place insufficiently fenced, or in a field adjoining a highway unless that field is so fenced or situate that animals therein cannot in any manner come in contact with any horse, ass, or mule passing along that highway or grazing on the sides thereof ;

(vi.) to graze a diseased horse, ass, or mule on a pasture being on the sides of a highway ; or

(vii.) to allow a diseased horse, ass, or mule to stray on the highway or thoroughfare or on the sides thereof, or on common or unenclosed land, or in a field or place insufficiently fenced.

(2). Where a horse, ass, or mule is exposed or otherwise dealt with in contravention of this Article, the Inspector of the Local Authority or other officer appointed by them in that behalf shall seize and remove and detain it, and the Local Authority shall cause it to be slaughtered with all practicable speed.

(3.) In case of a diseased horse, ass, or mule being seized in accordance with the provisions of this Article, that portion of the market or other place where the diseased horse, ass, or mule was found, shall not be used or allowed to be used for horses, asses, or mules by the market authority or the owner or occupier of the premises, unless and until a Veterinary Inspector has certified that that portion has been, as far as practicable, cleansed and disinfected.

(4). The Local Authority may recover the expenses of the execution by them or by their Inspector or other officer of the provisions of this Article from the owner of the horse, ass, or mule seized, or from the consignor or consignee thereof, either of whom may recover the same from the owner in any court of competent jurisdiction.

Restriction on Movement of Animals, Carcases, Dung, &c.

15.—(1.) It shall not be lawful for any person to send or carry, or cause to be sent or carried, on a railway, canal, river, or inland navigation, or in a coasting vessel, or on a highway or thoroughfare, any dung, fodder, or litter that has been in any place in contact with or used about a diseased horse, ass, or mule, except with a Licence of the Local Authority for the District in which such place is situate, granted on a certificate of an Inspector of the Local Authority certifying that the thing moved has been, as far as practicable, disinfected.

(2.) A Local Authority may cause or allow a diseased horse, ass, or mule or a carcase of any such animal to be taken into the District of another Local Authority to be destroyed or buried, with the previous consent of that Local Authority, or with a Licence in that behalf of the Board, but not otherwise.

Special Provision as to movement of Diseased Horses, Asses, or Mules for slaughter.

16.—(1.) Notwithstanding anything in this Order, a Local Authority may cause any horse, ass, or mule liable to be slaughtered by them under this Order to be moved in a properly constructed float or van to the premises of a person licensed to slaughter horses or other place convenient for such slaughter.

(2.) Any float or van, which has been used for the conveyance of any diseased horse, ass, or mule, shall immediately after each occasion of such use be cleansed and disinfected by and at the expense of the Local Authority as follows:

(i.) The floor of the float or van and all other parts thereof with which the horse, ass, or mule, or its droppings, have come in contact shall be scraped and swept, and the scrapings and sweepings, and all dung, sawdust, litter, and other matter shall be effectually removed therefrom; then

(ii.) The same parts of the float or van shall be thoroughly washed or scrubbed or scoured with water; then

(iii.) The same parts of the float or van shall be disinfected in one of the modes prescribed by Article one Diseases of Animals (Disinfection) Order of 1906.

(3.) The scrapings and sweepings of the float or van, and all dung, sawdust, litter, and other matter removed therefrom, shall forthwith be well mixed with quicklime, and be effectually removed from contact with animals.

Disposal of Carcases.

17.—(1.) The carcase of every horse, ass, or mule that was diseased at the time when it died, and of every animal slaughtered under this Order, shall be disposed of by the Local Authority as follows:

(i.) Either the Local Authority shall cause the carcase to be buried as soon as possible in its skin in some proper place, and to be covered with a sufficient quantity of quicklime or other disinfectant, and with not less than six feet of earth;

(ii.) Or the Local Authority may, if authorised by the Licence of the Board, cause the carcase to be destroyed, under the inspection of the Local Authority, in the mode following: The carcase shall be disinfected, and shall then be taken, in charge of an officer of the Local Authority, to premises approved for the purpose by the Board, and shall be there destroyed by exposure to a high temperature, or by chemical agents;

(iii.) Or the carcase may be disposed of in any other manner authorised by Licence of the Board.

(2.) With a view to the execution of the foregoing provisions of this Article the Local Authority may make such Regulations as they think fit for prohibiting or regulating the removal of any such carcase, or for securing the burial or destruction of the same.

(3.) Where under this Article a Local Authority cause a carcase to be buried, they shall first cause its skin to be so slashed as to be useless.

Digging up.

18. It shall not be lawful for any person, except with the Licence of an Inspector of the Board, to dig up, or cause to be dug up, the carcase of any horse, ass, or mule that has been buried.

Weekly Returns as to Disease.

19.—When an Inspector of a Local Authority finds glanders or farcy in his District, he shall forthwith make a return thereof to the Local Authority and to the Board, on a form provided by the Board, with all particulars therein required, and shall continue so to make a return thereof on the Saturday of every week until the disease has ceased.

General Provisions as to Regulations of Local Authority.

20.—(1.) Every Local Authority shall forthwith send to the Board two copies of every Regulation made by them under this Order.

(2.) If the Board are satisfied on inquiry with respect to any Regulation of a Local Authority made under this Order that the same is of too restrictive a character, or otherwise objectionable, and direct the revocation thereof, the same shall thereupon cease to operate.

(3.) The power to make Regulations under this Order shall be exercised only by the Local Authority or their Executive Committee and shall not be deputed to any other Committee or Sub-Committee.

Extension of certain Sections of Diseases of Animals Act, 1894.

21. Horses, asses, and mules shall be animals, and glanders (including farcy) shall be a disease, for the purposes of the following sections of the Act of 1904 (namely) :
Sections nineteen and twenty (slaughter and compensation) ;
Section forty-three (powers of police) ;
Section forty-four (powers of inspectors) ;
Section forty-five (detention of vessels) ;
and also for the purposes of all other sections of the said Act containing provisions relative to or consequent on the provisions of those sections and this Order, including such sections as relate to offences or procedure.

Exemption of Army Veterinary Department and Veterinary Colleges.

22.—Nothing in this Order applies to horses, asses, or mules in stables of military barracks or camps or in vessels, if the animals are under the care and supervision of the Army Veterinary Department, or to horses, asses, or mules in stables of any Veterinary College affiliated to the Royal College of Veterinary Surgeons : Provided that nothing in this Article shall be deemed to apply to the carcase of any horse, ass, or mule, nor to exempt a Local Authority from any obligation imposed on them in regard to the disposal of carcases.

Offences.

23.—(1.) If any horse, ass or mule is landed in contravention of this Order, the owner thereof, and the owner and the lessee and the occupier of the place of landing where such animal is landed, and also the owner and the charterer and the master of the vessel from which the same is landed, shall, each according to and in respect of his own acts and defaults, be deemed guilty of an offence against the Act of 1894.

(2.) If any horse, ass, or mule, or the carcase of any horse, ass, or mule, is moved in contravention of this Order, or of a Regulation or Notice under this Order, the owner of such horse, ass, or mule, or carcase, and the person for the time being in charge thereof, and the person causing, directing, or permitting the movement, and the person moving or conveying such horse, ass, or mule, or carcase, and the owner and the charterer and the master of the vessel in which it is moved, and the consignee or other person receiving or keeping it knowing it to have been moved in contravention as aforesaid, shall, each according to and in respect of his own acts and defaults, be deemed guilty of an offence against the Act of 1894.

(3.) If anything is omitted to be done as regards cleansing or disinfection in contravention of this Order or of a Regulation of a Local Authority made under this Order, the owner and the lessee and the occupier of any place or thing in or in respect of which—and the person using the van, cart, or other vehicle in which—(as the case may be) the same is omitted, shall, each according to and in respect of his own acts and defaults, be deemed guilty of an offence against the Act of 1894.

Interpretation.

24. In this Order—

"The Board" means the Board of Agriculture and Fisheries:

"The Act of 1894" means the Diseases of Animals Act, 1894:

"Inspector" includes Veterinary Inspector:

"Owner" includes an authorised agent of an owner:

"Carcase" means the carcase of a horse, ass, or mule, and part of such a carcase, and the flesh, bones, skin, hoofs, offal, or other part of a horse, ass, or mule separately or otherwise, or any portion thereof:

Other terms have the same meaning and scope as in the Act of 1894.

Revocation.

25. The Order described in the Second Schedule to this Order is hereby from and after the commencement of this Order revoked.

Existing Regulations.

26. Any Regulation made by a Local Authority under the Order revoked by this Order, or under any previous Order, and in force at the commencement of this Order, shall, except as hereinafter provided, remain in force unless altered or revoked by the Local Authority, for such time and in such manner as if this Order had not been made, and for the purposes of this Order shall be deemed to have been made under this Order: Provided that any such regulation which relates to the movement of horses, asses, or mules is hereby revoked.

Extent.

27. This Order extends to England and Wales and Scotland.

Local Authority to enforce Order.

28. The provisions of this Order, except where it is otherwise provided, shall be executed and enforced by the Local Authority.

Commencement.

29. This Order shall come into operation on the first day of January, nineteen hundred and eight.

Short Title.

30. This Order may be cited as the GLANDERS OR FARCY ORDER OF 1907.

In witness whereof the Board of Agriculture and Fisheries have hereunto set their Official Seal this twenty-third of August, nineteen hundred and seven.

T. H. ELLIOTT,
Secretary.

APPENDIX—GLANDERS IN MAN.

I hope I shall not be misunderstood for adding a note on this subject. I certainly have no wish to usurp the place of the medical man, but a special experience has forced upon me the danger of the disease to those connected with horses, and the frequency with which its recognition is overlooked. The symptoms of glanders are more definite in the horse than in man, and yet veterinarians know too well the difficulty of diagnosis which prevailed before mallein became available as an aid.

In man, glanders appears in two forms, acute and chronic, but either may be a sequel of the other. When acute glanders does not cause death in three or four weeks the patient may linger on with the chronic form, showing itself by more or less active lesions which sometimes heal but more often reappear in different parts of the body. A very few cases seem to recover.

The period of incubation in man is usually short—from 2 to 6 days. There are recorded cases in which symptoms have not appeared until months after the patient has ceased to have any connection with horses, and these are probably cases in which the disease has run a latent course.

The symptoms of an acute case are high fever, headache, and pains in the limbs. These may be the only manifestations of disease for a week or more, and then a cutaneous rash appears, in the form of nodules which rapidly break down into ulcers. Frequently this rash is not visible till a day, or two days, before death, and the patient dies of an acute septic-aemia with few or no local lesions.

I quote some reported cases showing how protean are the forms of human glanders.

i. Inquest on George Chinn, at Lambeth, December 12th, 1905. The man was a farrier, and worked in a cab-yard. Returned home on November 21st and said to his wife, "I've got glanders." She saw blood and matter from his nose. Dr. Councell was called in on the 24th. He saw no blood or matter. The patient complained of general malaise, but there were no localised symptoms. The witness noticed haemorrhagic spots on both legs upward as far as the knees, and a foul ulcer on the right forearm. In the absence of other signs, witness came to the conclusion that he was suffering from septic absorption in consequence of this foul ulcer.

On November 29th the patient was admitted to St. Thomas' Hospital, and was seen by Dr. Dean on December 3rd, who said his temperature was 103 and his pulse very rapid. On the hard palate and on the tongue were greenish-yellow patches. The legs were covered by large haemorrhagic patches. The patient was not admitted for glanders, and the disease was not at that time considered. Owing to the haemorrhagic spots which appeared from day to day, the physician in charge came to the conclusion that it was a case of glanders. The man died on the 8th.

ii. Inquest on Albert Tharby, at the London Hospital early in September, 1905. The man was a carman, and felt unwell on August 5th. Treated by Dr. Sergeant at his surgery daily till the 10th. On the 13th Doctor visited him at his house. Found large red spot on each keee, with pain in the joints. Said the case was one of septic pneumonia, and patient had better go to hospital, which he did next day. Died on August 30th. Verdict: death from glanders. This man only drove one horse; did not clean or feed any others. The horse he drove was tested with mallein, and gave no reaction.

iii. Two cases reported in the "*Lancet*" by Dr. Goodall. A man, aged fifty-five, a printer, was admitted into the Eastern Fever Hospital, on October 28th, 1903. He had been seized with shivering and pain in the limbs on the 9th. On the 11th he was worse, and was medically attended at home till the 20th. On that date he went as out-patient to a general hospital, whence he was sent as a case of typhoid fever to the Eastern Hospital. On admission he was semi-comatose. On the skin were a number of small superficial pustules, most abundant on the chest, right leg, and right forearm. There were a few on the left cheek, the back, left thigh, and left upper arm. Besides these pustules there were several swellings of varying size in different places—one on the right frontal eminence, two on the right forearm, two on the left forearm, one on the right leg, and one on the left. The largest swelling fluctuated, the smaller did not. Some appeared to be in the subcutaneous tissue, others were distinctly in muscles. There was no discharge from the nose. On the morning of the 30th, the contents of a swelling on the right leg were drawn off and microscopically examined. A bacillus resembling that of glanders was at once detected. The patient died on the 31st.

The second case was that of a stableman, who was taken ill with "pains all over him," ten days before admission. He was sent to a general hospital as a case of blood-poisoning, and then to the Eastern Hospital as one of typhoid fever. In one of the muscles of the left forearm was a nodular swelling. The left knee-joint was much swollen, very painful, and distended with fluid. The patient said that the lump in the arm had been present since February 18th and the knee-joint had been affected since the 16th. Next day an examination of fluid from the knee and arm was made, but no organisms were found. Cultivations in agar were made; and, on the second day, what appeared to be the bacillus mallei was detected. A day or two later, Drs. Lewis and Wood obtained the bacillus from the fluid of the knee-joint. The patient died delirious on March 11th.

iv. An inquest was held at Westminster, on August 15th, on Albert Allen, a horse-keeper in an omnibus yard. Dr. Cope saw the patient first on June 12th, when he showed symptoms of an ordinary cold, with aching of the limbs. He was treated for a rheumatic attack. On the 19th there was a nodule on the leg, and some inflammation of the limb. On July 12th other nodules appeared on the right arm, and on the 13th the man was taken to Westminster Hospital.

Mr. Frank Mott saw him on the 14th; and, as there was a suspicion of glanders, some pus was examined, and the bacillus mallei discovered. The man died August 11th. An autopsy revealed eleven abscesses scattered over the arms and legs. There was pus in the knee-joint. Nothing was found in the nose, throat, larynx, or trachea; but in the lungs some small nodules, about the size of a pea, were discovered.

v. In a note published by Drs. Bullock and Twort, the London Hospital, the first sentence is: "Glanders in man is generally believed to be uncommon, although, no doubt, the belief is partially due to the protean characters which the disease manifests clinically, and which render it difficult of diagnosis." They then give details of six cases which had come under their notice at the hospital, and of a seventh case which was of doubtful character. Four of these cases were chronic, and characterised by recurring abscesses which lasted for months.

vi. Inquest on Charles Nicholls, a horse-keeper, at Westminster, May 19th, 1905. On May 1st the man complained of illness, and saw a doctor, who said he had pleurisy. Two or three days later he was taken to St. George's Hospital, where he died on the 16th. Dr. Hunt said he diagnosed the case as rheumatic fever. Dr. Ethrington, house-physician, said the deceased, on admission, seemed to be suffering from rheumatic fever. The day before death it was thought to be glanders, and a post-mortem examination verified the diagnosis.

vii. From "*The Lancet*" of April, I take the following from a Report by Mr. M. J. Cromie, House-Surgeon, Westminster Hospital. A horse-keeper, aged twenty-five, was admitted on November 12th, 1904. A consultation between Dr. Hebb and Mr. Spencer led to a surmise that the patient was suffering from glanders. On the following day Dr. Hebb found the bacillus mallei. The patient died thirty-three hours after admission. "A full consideration of the case exposes possibilities of infection, and of such cases being overlooked" is Mr. Cromie's comment, and the history more than bears this out. On November 3rd he had pain and swelling of the left side of face, and was advised by a dentist to bathe his face in hot water, as an abscess was forming. He next saw two other medical men, who told him that he had cellulitis and erysipelas. On the 9th, small hard lumps began to appear in the neighbourhood of the joints, with pain in the joints, especially the knees. On this day the patient went to a hospital, and on his out-patient paper was entered "cellulitis of the face." An incision was advised; but, as he could not be admitted and felt very ill, he declined it. On the 10th, the nodular swellings became red and inflamed, and pustules appeared on the swollen face, the lips, and the buccal aspects of the lips and cheek. The lips became black, nasal discharge commenced, and dyspnoea supervened. He was therefore taken to another hospital, when he was given a paper, saying he was suffering from cellulitis and cephalitis (*sic.*). Finally, he was taken in an ambulance to the Westminster Hospital.

The post-mortem examination showed abscesses in the muscles all over the body. The mucosa of the nose and sinuses was much swollen, but there was no ulceration of the nasal membrane. The lungs were engorged, and the seat of numerous abscesses.

viii. An inquest was held at Ipswich on September 26th, on Edward Rogers, an ostler. On September 5th he received a wound on his right hand in balling some horses. On the 12th he went to work at another stable, but in two days the arm became swollen, and he attended as an out-patient at the Hospital. Dr. Rygate then attended, and treated the case as one of blood-poisoning, till the 23rd, when a consultation was held with the Medical Officer of Health, and the man taken to the Fever Hospital. He died delirious on Sunday, the 25th.

No post-mortem examination was made, which is unfortunate, as the case was one of direct inoculation, and some description of the lymphatic glands of the injured limb would have been helpful.

ix. On May 14th, 1903, an inquest was held at the Town Hall, Chelsea, on Charles Ford, an organ-grinder. The man kept his organ in a mews, but lived in a street some distance off. A case of glanders existed in a stable opposite that in which the organ was kept, about a month previous to the man being taken ill, and the mews had frequently contained glandered horses. The widow said " It was about a month since he first complained of pains in his head and all over his body." Dr. Cope was called in, and treated the case as one of influenza. He had no cuts or sores about him, as far as she knew. He was taken to the Infirmary on April 28th. Dr. Coulson, Assistant-Medical Superintendent at St. George's Workhouse Infirmary, said the man was admitted for debility after influenza. He had a high temperature, but no local symptoms until three days before death. Then a small sore developed over the left eye. The next day there was suppuration from the nose. The post-mortem examination disclosed several small nodules on the skin of the face and nose. The nasal membrane was intact, as was that of the larynx and trachea. Thick tenacious pus was found under the dura mater. A deep-seated swelling on the left forearm, on being incised, was found to be an intra-muscular abscess.

x. An inquest was held at Hammersmith, in November, 1893, on William Wallace, a horse-keeper. The widow stated that towards the end of September the deceased told her he had been bitten by a horse, and about a week later he complained of severe headache. Following this came pain in the arms and legs, and on October 7th he went to a dispensary. The pains increased, and on October 14th he went to West London Hospital, when he was told that he was suffering from rheumatic fever. He was admitted into the Hospital on the 18th, and died on the 24th. Dr. Wilks, the House-Physician, said the case was of a very doubtful character, and it was not till the 23rd that a diagnosis of glanders was made.

I think it may be concluded from these cases that two symptoms which have been trusted to are not often prominent—a recognised spot at which inoculation has taken place, and the nasal ulceration and discharge. The symptoms which are most suggestive are—the combination of high fever, a cutaneous rash, and pains in the muscles and joints.

Chronic glanders has been brought rather prominently into notice by Dr. Bullock, who described six cases diagnosed bacteriologically at the London Hospital. But the whole subject has been treated very fully by Dr. Robins of the Royal Victoria Hospital, Montreal, in a monograph of about 100 pages. He has collected from French, English and German periodicals, notes of 156 cases of chronic glanders, which he has analysed most thoroughly. From synopsis of these I venture to copy a few as evidence of the variations in the symptoms of the disease which make it so difficult to diagnose.

Travers's 1st case. (Travers, Inquiry into Constitutional Irritation, quoted by Elliotson, Medico-Chirurgical Transactions, XVI, 1830, 171.)

Veterinary student, injured hand dissecting glandered donkey. Lymphangitis of arm, abscesses, suppuration in lungs, knee joints and kidney; hectic fever. Two donkeys—positive. Duration not stated. Died.

Sédillot. (Reported to Academy of Sciences (Paris) October 11, 1847, abstr. in London Med. Times, XVII, 1847—48, 35.)

Soldier, 26, groomed several glandered horses. Malaise, 'ague,' abscesses of extremities, cough, diarrhoea, caries of head bones, gangrenous ulceration of throat and larynx, phlegmon. Three horses inoculated developed glanders. Two years. Died. Lobular abscesses of lungs, spleen, liver; ulceration of trachea, purulent thrombosis of saphena vein.

Note statement that the unhealthy aspect assumed by the wounds of several other patients when washed with sponges used by this patient, cleared up all doubt as to the nature and contagious character of the disorder.

Hallopeau and Jeanselme. (Ann. de Dermatol. et de Syphilographie, série 3, II, 1891, 273. Vide also Brit. Journ. of Dermatol, 1893, 250.)

A Carter, 24, cared for glandered horse. Fever, nasal discharge, joint pains, multiple stubborn abscesses; apparent cure three years; fresh abscesses, swelling of lacrymal sacs, ulceration of nose, palate and lips, septum perforated, phlegmon and pustules of face, conjunctivitis, diarrhoea, jaundice, albuminuria, foetid diarrhoea, ascites. B. Mallei. Donkey and guinea pigs—positive. Antisyphilitics useless. Six years. Died.

Holmes (Journ. American Med. Assoc. XXI, 1893, 234.)

Farmer, 22, treated two glandered horses. Felon of finger, multiple abscesses, edges sometimes covered with shotty granulations, bone involvement, adenitis; sharp stinging pain first localised the foci. Guinea pig—positive. Prompt excision or cauterization immediately foci were localised by the occurrence of sharp, stinging pain. Two and a half years.

Definite cure. Well over a year later. Note stinging pain marking onset of foci, probably due to embolism, shotty granulations on edges of abscesses, and success following persistent radical surgical treatment—20 operations under general anaesthesia in two and a half years.

Nencki and Pruszynski. (Gazeta Legarsha, 1896, 268, quoted by von Baracz, Virchow's Archiv., CLIX, 490 et seq.)

Physician, origin of disease not stated. Chills, pains in legs, a few abscesses, pains over left kidney, suppuration of left knee. B. Mallei found, and guinea pig—positive. In this case, the physician who infected finger operating on knee of patient died of acute glanders. Potassium iodide. Six months. Died.

Jenckel. (Deutsches Ztschr. f. Chir., LXXVI, 1904, 130.)

Pathological assistant, helped at human glanders autopsy while finger wound. Lymphangitis of arm, asthenia, suppuration of epitrochlear gland with limited phlegmon about lesion. B. Mallei in pure culture. Guinea-pig—positive. Six weeks. Definite cure, well, four years later.

Incubation seven days; numerous previous ordinary wound infections had never weakened the patient to a similar extent, nor had they ever caused suppuration of epitrochlear gland.

Cope. (London Veterinary Record, Aug. 19th, 1905, 143.)

Stableman, 45. Employers denied glanders among horses, but four were in isolation, at inquest. No known abrasion; ordinary cold, and aching limbs, nodule and phlegmon of leg, weakness, emaciation, fever, slight abscesses of extremities, including kneejoint. B. Mallei. Over two months. Died. Pea-sized pulmonary nodules, especially in left lower lobe; signs of septicaemia.

Schilling. (Rust's Magazin f. die gesammte Heilkunde, XI, 1821, 480. Quoted by Elliotson, Medico-Chirurgical Transactions, XVI, 1830, 171.)

Soldier, 34, washed noses of glandered horses. Rheumatic pains, phlegmon and gangrene of face, pustular rash on forehead, arms and legs; offensive nasal discharge. Seven weeks. Died. Gelatinous masses in tissues (thymus region), abscesses in muscles.

Generally considered the first indubitable case of human glanders published.

Bouley. Tardieu (Thèse de Paris, 1043, abstr. in Arch. de Méd. Expérimentale, 1897, 144.)

Veterinary surgeon, 26, cut finger during autopsy on glandered horse. Multiple abscesses, cauterized with red-hot iron. Sixteen months. Definite cure. Lived 45 years after. Incubation 15 days.

Williams and Taylor. (Dublin Med. Press, XXVII, 1852, 212.)

Hackney carman, 51, treated several glandered horses, injecting their nostrils. After healing of slight injury to skin a local rash appeared at once, cough (pharyngeal) expectoration, nasal discharge, eyes suffused, pustular rash, phlegmon and slight gangrene of face. Seven months. Died. Autopsy showed that his horse had typical glanders.

Finzi. (London Veterinary Record, Oct. 20th, 1894, 237.)

Cabman, 53, lacerated thumb wound, from kick of glandered horse, refused to heal. Fever, nodules and abscesses in extremities; pustular rash on face, scalp and limbs, delirium, vomiting and diarrhoea. Over six weeks. Died. Lungs thickly studded with deposits.

———

It is not my intention, or my province, to enter upon any full description of glanders in man. If it were, there is a large amount of interesting material in Dr. Robins' monograph, from which I should like to make lengthy extracts. This study of chronic glanders in man, is the most complete and thorough I have read, and deserves wide recognition. I cannot refrain from one more extract from it :—" There is reason to think that, wherever horses are, glanders may, and as a matter of fact does, exist. Every continent has furnished cases. Judging from the cases reported, it would seem that the disease is at the present time, most prevalent in Cuba, and in some of the countries of Europe, particularly Russia. But there is reason to believe that the disease among men is much more prevalent, in other countries as well as those mentioned, than is generally supposed, or than might be inferred from a study of the number of cases reported in medical literature........It is probable that hundreds of cases annually find their way into the mortality records of the civilized countries of the world, classified as typhoid, pyaemia, erysipelas, tuberculosis, syphilis, etc., which should properly be put down to glanders."

It is remarkable how seldom any direct evidence of inoculation through the skin is given in recorded cases of human glanders, although a wound is always expected and looked for. I venture to suggest that too much credence has been given to the idea that man is generally infected by inoculation.

Horses are almost always infected by ingestion of contaminated food, and there seems no reason to believe that a similar method of infection, may not take place in man. The habits of some stablemen are careless in the extreme, and I have frequently had to tell men who had handled the pus-covered nostril of a glandered horse to go and wash their hands. They were quite satisfied to wipe the contaminated hand on the seat of their trousers, and then to resume their meal of bread and beef, or bread and cheese.

Experimental inoculation of glanders through the skin, and accidental infection of a wound, always cause local primary sores, and usually some lesions of the nearest lymphatic vessels and glands. We might expect that inoculation of the face and hands of man, if it occurred, would give rise to local lesions, and we know in cases where the wound and its infection are evident that marked local lesions do occur. The eruption that appears on man, usually a day, or two before death, soon forms sores or ulcers, but these lesions are secondary, and their occurence on the face does not prove that they indicate the site of inoculation. The ten days illness which often precedes any local lesion must have been due to glanders infection, and any inoculated spot would have given evidence of morbid change at least as early as the access of the febrile symptoms. The fever, high temperature and muscular pains which exist for days before a skin lesion appears, are, to me, evidence of infection through ingestion.

The larger Carnivora have been infected through eating the raw flesh of glandered horses. Man has undoubtedly consumed glandered flesh, and no consequent infection in him has ever been traced, but we may assume that he cooked his food and thus destroyed the bacilli.

There is positive evidence of glanders being conveyed to man by inoculation, there is strong negative evidence that many cases are due to ingestion, but there is no evidence of any infection by inhalation. If inspiration of air could convey glanders to man, it is impossible to believe that horsekeepers who spent twelve hours a day in stables full of glandered horses could possibly have escaped infection and death. Thirty years ago there were many stables in which all the horses were glandered, and yet infection of man was seldom seen. Infection through inhalation was a plausible theory when the nasal and lung lesions were thought to be the primary sores.

Glanders in man is such a loathsome and fatal disease as to deserve more attention than it receives. Probably if all cases were recognised, the mortality would be equally heavy, but prevention would be more actively assisted. If the medical profession called for the suppression of glanders as loudly as they did for the extermination of rabies, prevention in all animals would be accelerated. Hydrophobia in man ceased when we had stamped out rabies in dogs, and glanders in man will only cease when the disease no longer exists among horses.

Glanders has recently been scheduled as an industrial disease, and payment of compensation to infected employées by the owner of diseased horses follows. This ought to be more widely known, and the fact would lead to greater care.

The Glanders Order of 1907 requires notification by the local inspectors to the Medical Officer of Health of the district in which the disease is found.   This regulation is of little value, as any infection of man has taken place before the notification is served. If the M.O.H. forwarded his information to the medical practioners in his district, it might do some good by directing their attention to possible infections, and thus perhaps lead to an early diagnosis of other cases in man.

Finally, I would suggest that Glanders should be included in the list of human diseases which are subject to compulsory notification.

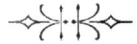

INDEX.

INDEX.

H. & W. BROWN, Printers, 20 Fulham Road, London, S.W.

PLATES.

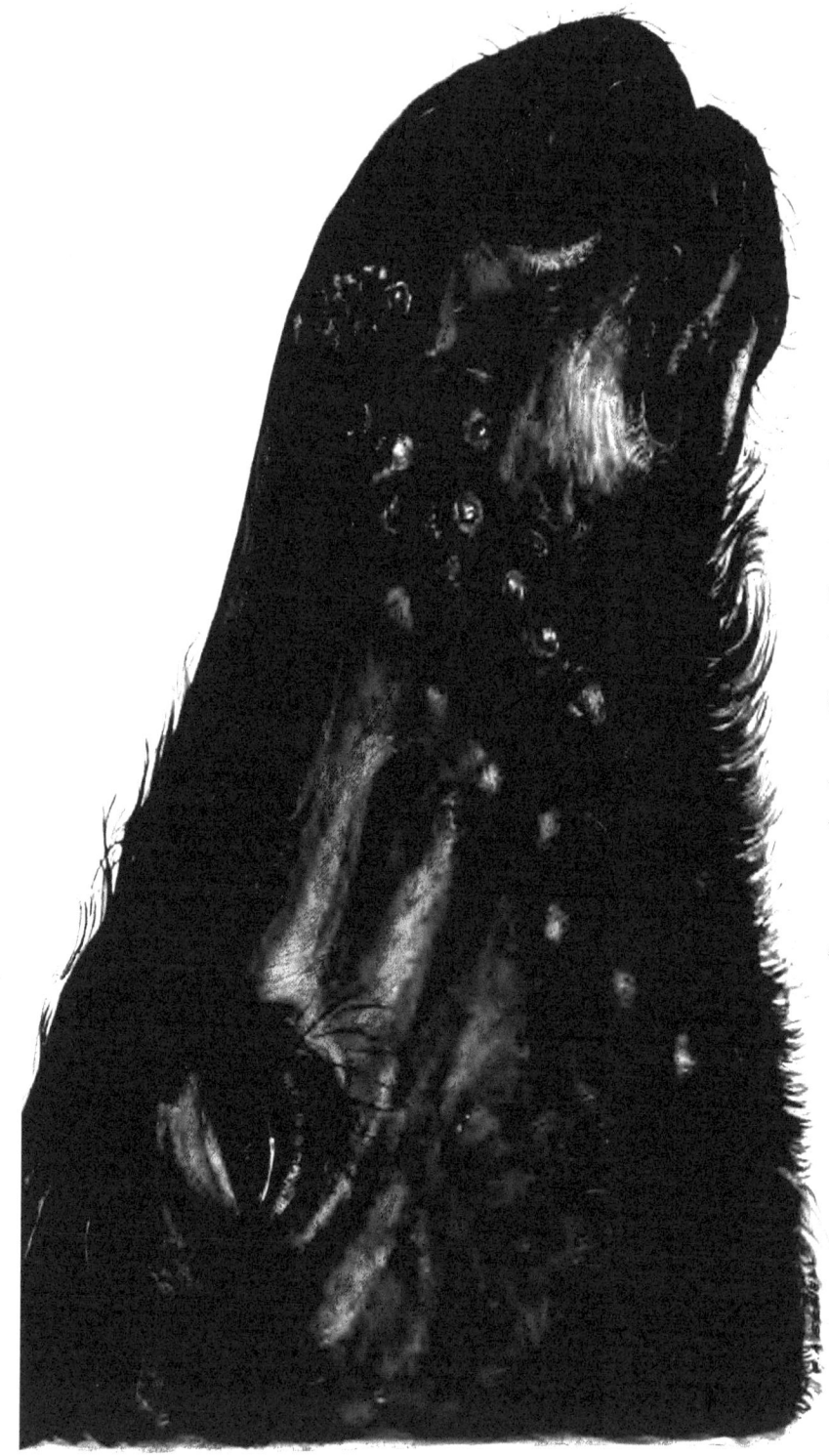

Cutaneous glanders. (Farcy). Showing broken and unbroken "buds."

Plate I.

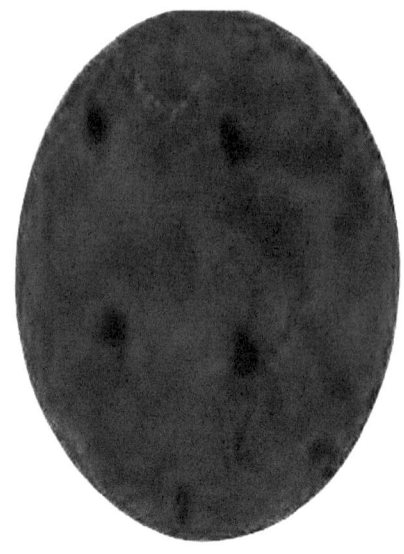

Dark spots showing position of nodules.

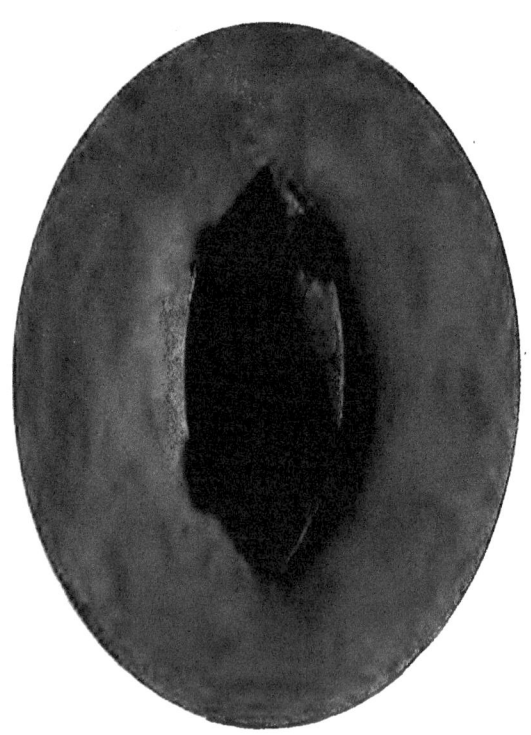

Section of early stage of pulmonary nodule.

Plate II.

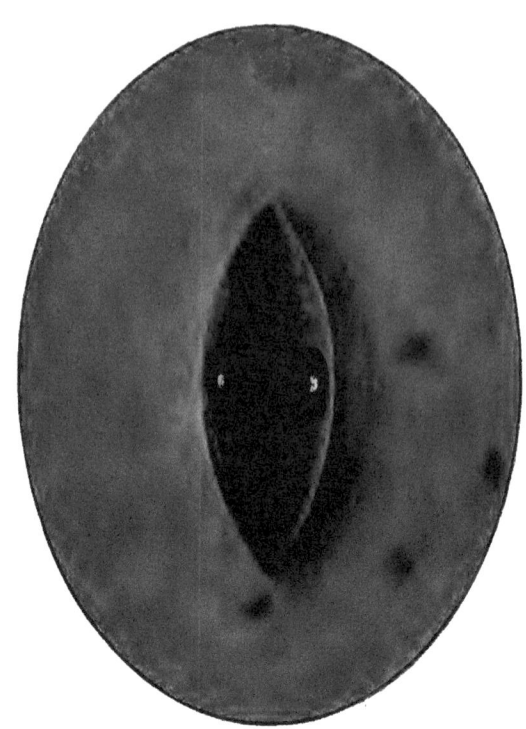

Section of medium aged pulmonary nodule,
showing lighter centre.

Section of lung, showing a larger lesion.

Section of pulmonary nodule completely caseated.

Plate III.

Portion of Spleen.
Three glanders nodules are visible on the surface.

Plate IV.

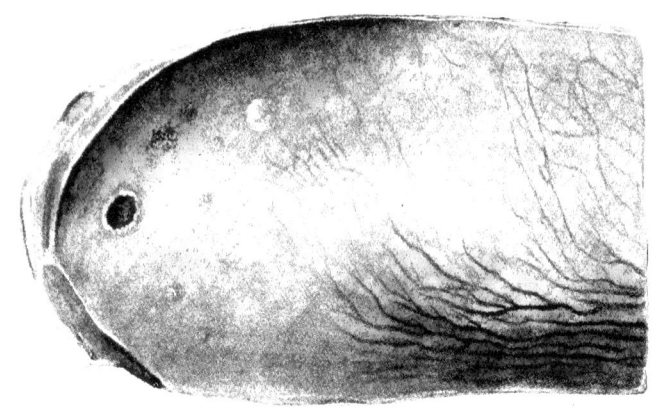

Septum. Lesions visible during life ulcers and vesicles.

Plate V.

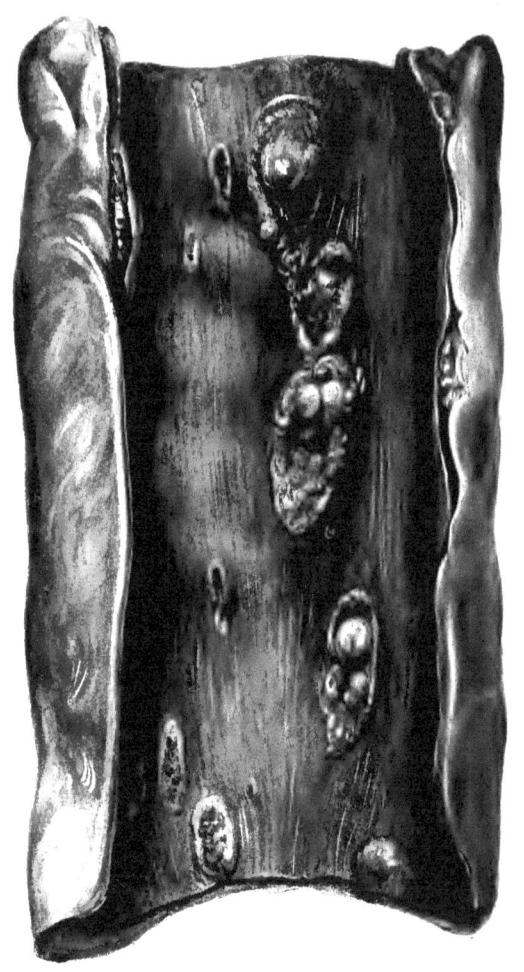

Portion of trachea, showing large ulcers.

Plate VI.

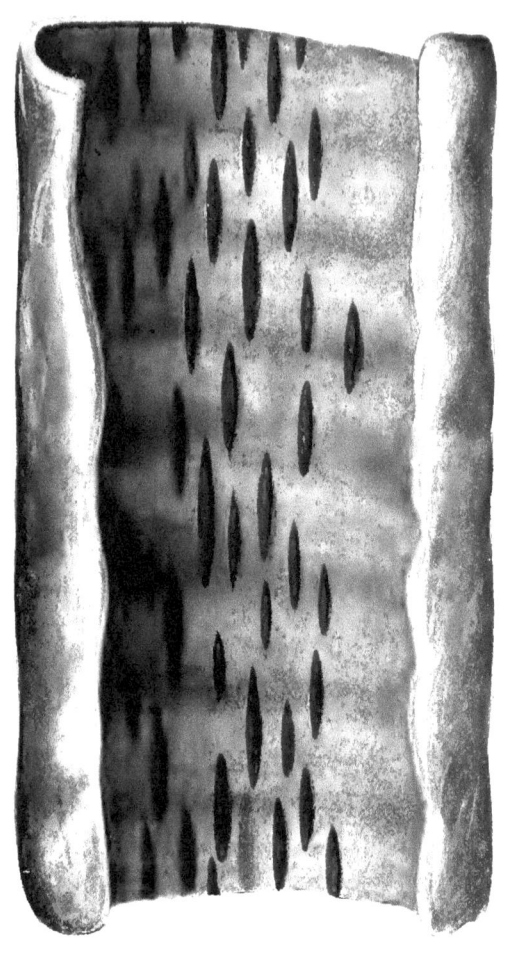

Portion of trachea, showing an early stage of ulceration,
found usually in mallein reactors.

Plate VII.

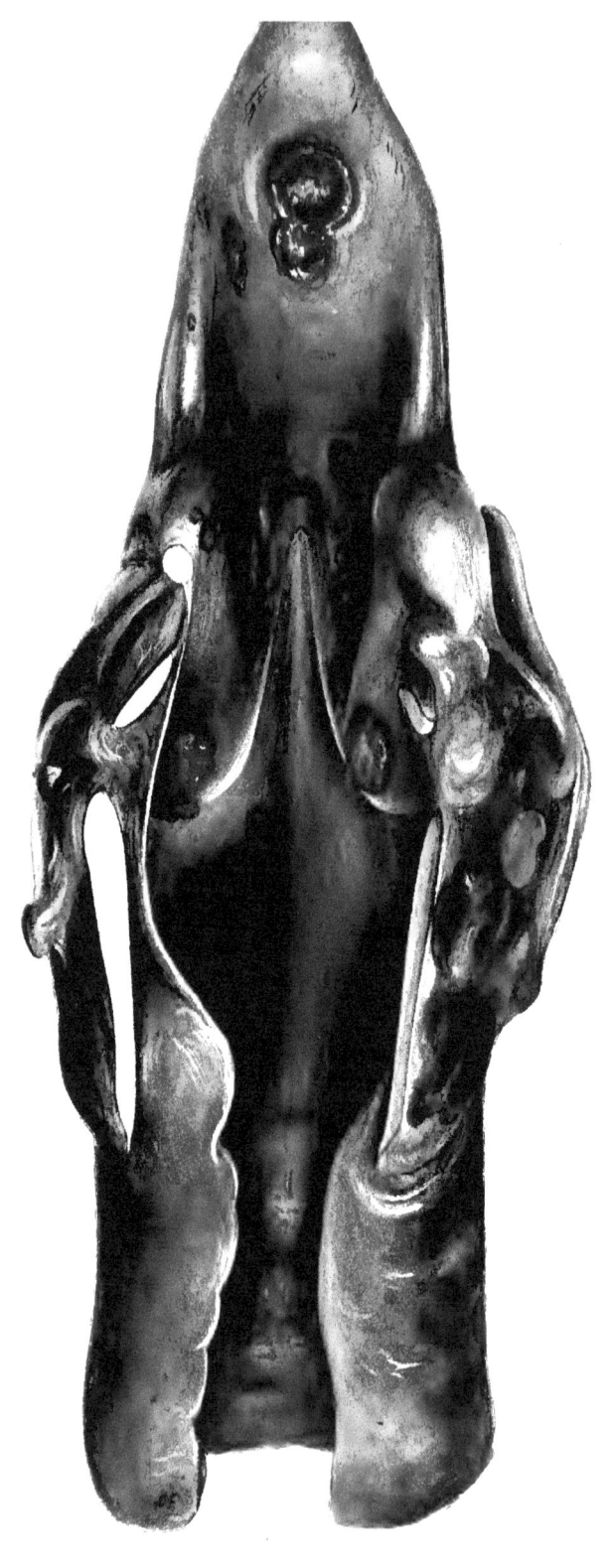

Ulcerated larynx, from unusually acute case.

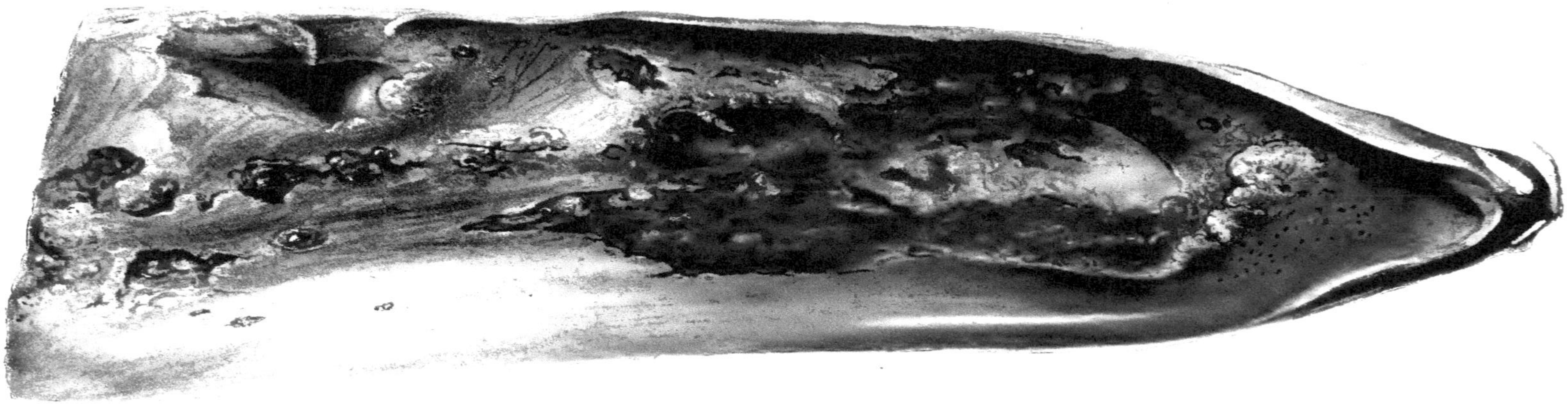

Septum. Unusually extensive ulceration.

Plate IX.

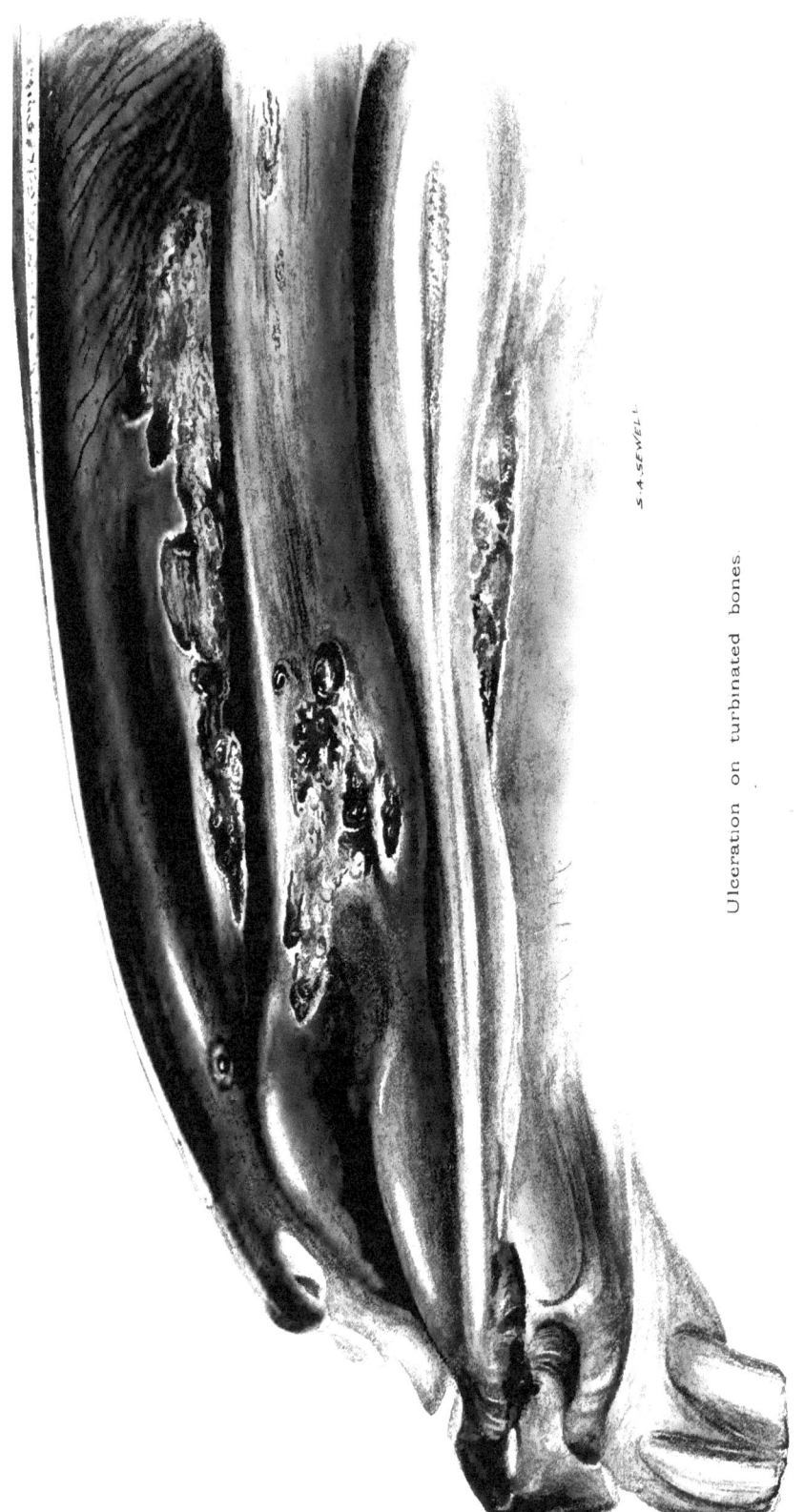

S.A.SEWELL

Ulceration on turbinated bones.

Plate X.

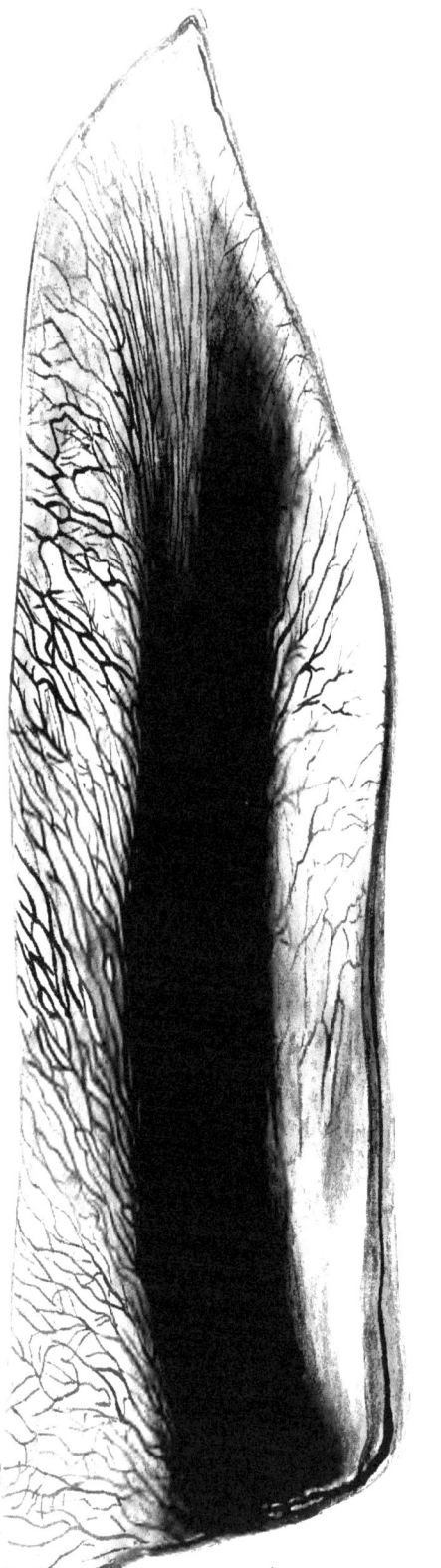

Septum showing exceptional infiltration. From a case of Farcy.

Plate XI.

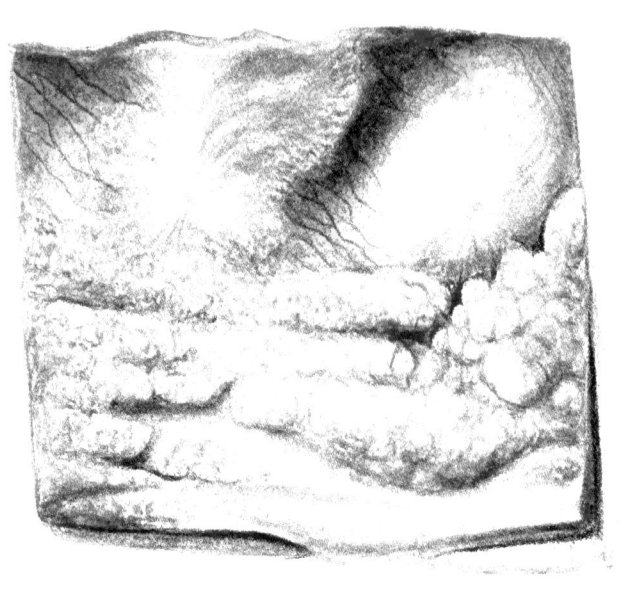

Portion of septum,
showing two cicatrices and a mass of granulation tissue.

Plate XII.

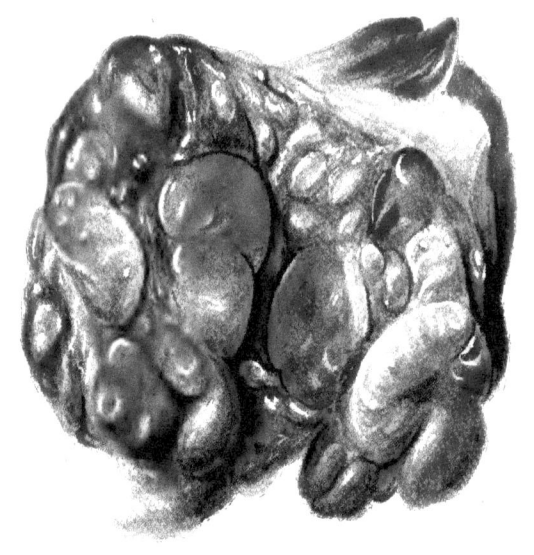

Sub-maxillary gland laid open,
showing numerous caseous centres.

Plate XIII.

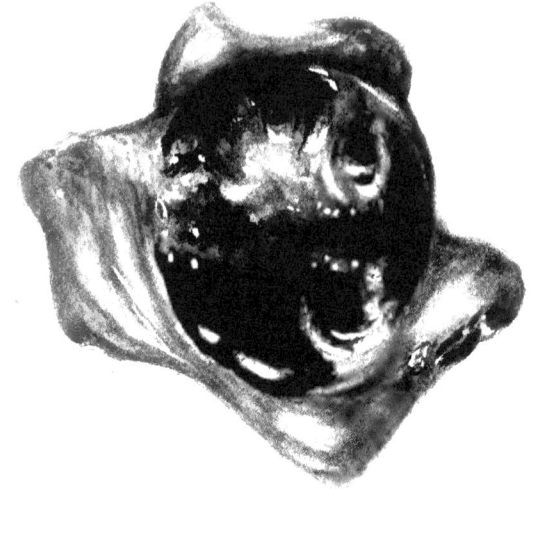

Bronchial gland, deeply pigmented,
showing numerous white caseous centres.

Plate XIV.

Sub-maxillary gland laid open, showing
caseous centres. In the lower part a
large calcified nodule, divided in sectioning

ImTheStory.com

Lightning Source UK Ltd.
Milton Keynes UK
UKHW02f1145131117

312661UK00007B/1100/P